W9-AYN-413

Once-a-Month Cooking

Cooking

REVISED AND EXPANDED

A Proven System for Spending Less Time in
the Kitchen and Enjoying Delicious,
Homemade Meals Every Day

MIMI WILSON and
MARY BETH LAGERBORG

St. Martin's Griffin ❧ New York

www.stmartins.com

Book design by Mary A. Wirth

LIBRARY OF CONGRESS CATALOGING-IN-PUBLICATION DATA

Wilson, Mimi, 1946–
    Once-a-month cooking : a proven system for spending less time in the kitchen and enjoying delicious,
homemade meals everyday / Mimi Wilson and Mary Beth Lagerborg.
        p. cm.
    ISBN-13: 978-0-312-36625-4
    ISBN-10: 0-312-36625-6
    1. Make-ahead cookery. 2. Frozen foods. I. Lagerborg, Mary Beth. II. Title.
    TX652.W566 2007
    641.5'55—dc22

                                                                    2006050616

First Edition: March 2007

10   9   8   7   6   5   4   3   2   1

Contents

ACKNOWLEDGMENTS

Special thanks to these friends who helped:

Debbie Lee

Renae Loring

Erica Rinde

Julie Luplow

Colette Compoz

Janae Martinez

Jennifer Stealing

Cori Peth

Rebecca Pasquariello

Anne Gates

Darran Metzler

Sue Herd

Cynthia Bahlman

Captain Lois True

Ginger Brown

Linnea Rein

Sandi Hanson

Cala Doolittle

Marge Rodemer

Alice Tate

Linda Strohkorb

Julie Witt

Once-a-Month Cooking

Introduction

"What's for dinner?" is the perennial, pesky question that has probably compelled you to open the pages of this book. You might have tonight covered, but what about tomorrow? Your family's need to eat—better yet, their need to eat together—comes in relentless waves. But, let's face it: You have better things to do than cook! So what can you do? Well, we're here to provide a solution.

Once-a-Month Cooking is a foolproof method of getting dinner on the table that's perfect for anyone who doesn't always want to cook, but who wishes they had something prepared and ready to go. You know your family well and you know that nothing unravels the seams of quality family time faster than having nothing on hand for dinner. Having an empty refrigerator or pantry gives everyone the grumps, forcing you to pile into the car and drive over to the local take-out place or fast-food restaurant. You generally sacrifice in nutrition, added expense, and a riskier stab at quality family time. Even storefront versions of the *Once-a-Month Cooking* plan can't beat the cost savings and flexibility of our time-tested system.

If you're getting nervous at this point, with visions of glistening roasted chickens, complex recipes that take hours, and a pile of dishes in your sink, don't. You don't need to be particularly well organized or a spectacular cook to try *Once-a-Month Cooking*. You don't even need a separate freezer. What we're going to show you is an easy method of cooking one month's or two weeks' worth of dinner entrées at a time and freezing them. People always ask us, "Does it work?" It's the question we've been asked most often, and we can say without hesitation, "It does!" Besides being a smart cooking method that gets everything ready in advance, it will also help you save a significant amount of money on your weekly food bills without scrimping on taste and variety.

We will take you by the hand and give you a shopping list and lots of direction. We'll tell you what size containers to freeze the food in (most meals will fit into freezer bags) and suggest what to serve with your entrées. When you're finished, gazing into your well-stocked freezer will be a near-spiritual experience. Afterward, on any given day you can cook from scratch if you want to, but if you don't have time— no problem. This is a great way to simplify your life, relieving it of the daily stress of what to fix for dinner.

The beauty of *Once-a-Month Cooking* is that it provides the convenience of a home meal replacement with the aroma, appeal, taste, nutrition, and cost-savings of home cooking. For the investment of one large grocery haul and a day of megacooking, you have a month's (or two weeks') entrées available on time each day with little effort on your part beyond heating a meal and steaming vegetables or tossing a salad. And you don't need to dash out for fast food or Chinese takeout, or go to the neighborhood deli.

This system will save you money. Convenience foods are costly. So are forays into the supermarket at 5:00 P.M. with two preschoolers. A list that began with four items yields a cart holding twenty-two, including Froot Loops and Big Chew gum. With *Once-a-Month Cooking* you will have one large shopping trip a month (or every two weeks); then you'll only have to shop perhaps once a week for fresh produce, breakfasts, and lunches.

A bonus from your day's cooking investment is your flexibility. Having guests is more fun when the main dish is ready in advance. Your family can still have a home-cooked meal even if you're busy, have a new baby at home, when the holidays approach, or if you are traveling. What a joy it is to be able to respond to the special needs of your family and others!

We all know that nutrition fares better when we aren't eating catch-as-catch-can. And if you or another family member is on a special diet, *Once-a-Month Cooking* is an excellent way to feed the rest of the tribe.

You may want to try the two-week plan rather than the one-month plan if you are cooking in bulk for the first time, or if your family is small (fewer than four people). In that case, two week's worth will last you three weeks, since you'll package it in smaller containers.

But the greatest benefit of *Once-a-Month Cooking* is that it gives you a better shot at pulling the family together—at least a few evenings a week—to disengage from the concerns of the world and engage with one another. A warm meal on a set table wafts the aroma of care and value to a family. As one mom said, "When the food is ready, and we're gathered at the table, the rest of the craziness doesn't seem to matter."

Home meal replacements make it too easy for a family to separate, grab the meal when each family member wants, and see to his or her own needs. *Once-a-Month Cooking* will help you have a meal to gather round, including the rich aromas that are a delightful accompaniment to home cooking. Share the kitchen chores as well as your mealtimes together.

Once we're at the table it's discouraging to fall into the same conversation ruts about work or teachers, or how a child has misbehaved today. With our own families and friends we've found it's helpful and fun to sometimes "put a question on the table." We ask a question that each person at the table must address, but for which there is no right or wrong answer, such as "What is the funniest thing you saw today?"; "What is your favorite room of our home and why?"; "If you were an animal rather than a person, what animal would you like to be?" We've included table-talk questions to prime the pump for you. Turn off the television, ignore the telephone, and enjoy what you will learn about one another.

Mimi Wilson devised this cooking system to meet the daily needs of a busy family who entertained often. In the years since then, we have been encouraged and sometimes amused by the many uses people have found for, as we call it, "the method." Here are some that stretch beyond the obvious feeding of a busy family. Perhaps they will expand your vision for how you can use the wealth of food you will soon have on hand.

- Freeze individual portions to stock the freezer of an elderly parent or friend.
- Develop this as an at-home business to serve busy, two-income families. A day-care provider uses *Once-a-Month Cooking* so that, for a fee, parents can pick up a dinner entrée with their child!
- Cook the method with friends in a church or community kitchen and use the entrées to take to families in crisis.
- Give entrées as a gift for a new mother or for a woman experiencing a difficult pregnancy.

We can't resist sharing our personal favorite application. On a visit to Peru, Mimi's husband Calvin, a family physician, was part of a medical team that trekked into the jungle to treat a group of people dying from their first-ever exposure to pneumonia. When the team needed additional food, Mimi took frozen entrées, packaged in Tupperware and wrapped in newspapers, to a nearby airstrip. The pilot flew over the team's campsite in the jungle and dropped the entrées to them. We call this one "Bombs Away."

We receive many letters (and phone calls on cooking day). Some users actually say the results have saved their marriages.

Whatever your impulse for trying *Once-a-Month Cooking*, we trust you'll find generous rewards for your day's cooking.

If you have used the previous edition of *Once-a-Month Cooking,* you will find more than forty new recipes in this edition, a new section on fresh vegetables to serve with your entrées, and general fine-tuning.

Let's get cooking!

1

Getting Ready: An Overview of the Once-a-Month Plan

This cooking method enables you to prepare either a month's or two weeks' main dishes at once and freeze them. It includes two choices of one-month cycles and three choices of two-week cycles. If you rotate among these, you can easily provide great mealtime variety. We suggest that you start with a cycle from the book to get used to the method. Then you can experiment with adding family-favorite recipes. Turn to chapter 9 for help in adapting the method to your own recipes.

Each of the menu cycles gives you a menu calendar that shows the month's entrées at a glance, a grocery shopping list, a list of staples you should have on hand (add to the grocery list any you don't have), a list of the containers you will need for freezing the entrées, step-by-step instructions for preparing the recipes in sequence on your cooking day, and finally the recipes themselves, in the order you will prepare them.

To serve an entrée, you will need to thaw the dish and heat it. While it is being heated, you can prepare a vegetable, salad, or perhaps a dessert to serve with it. The time-consuming preparation and cleanup is done all at once on your megacooking day!

Since many of the entrées can be frozen in freezer bags instead of bulkier hard-sided containers, even a month's cycle can be stored in the freezer section of your refrigerator.

Just make sure you make room by cleaning it out before your cooking day. Sooner or later we need to deal with those hard knots of leftovers anyway! Right after cooking day you will probably not have room in the refrigerator's freezer for things like ice cream and loaves of bread, but as you use entrées from the freezer you can add these to it.

The recipes in *Once-a-Month Cooking* come not from stainless-steel test kitchens, but have been tested numerous times in homes by cooks of varying skills. We have selected recipes we think your family will eat and enjoy. They were chosen for taste, variety, nutritional value, easily available ingredients, and how well they lend themselves to freezing.

You will find that the recipes vary in serving size. The average is 5 or 6 servings. Some serve 4; a few serve 12. Depending on the ages (and eating habits) of your children, if you have four or fewer family members, you may want to divide and freeze each larger-serving entrée in two or more meal-size portions. The largest recipes are great for serving to company or ensuring leftovers the following day.

You may find that the one-month menu cycle actually feeds your family for five or six weeks or more—particularly if you occasionally eat out or supplement your menu with dinner salads or easy meals like grilled meats and vegetables.

Chapter 8 provides creative ways to serve fresh seasonal vegetables and other accompaniments with your entrées—as well as a few sweet treats to have on hand in your freezer. We think you will be as excited as we are about the wealth of ideas presented by our friend Rebecca Pasquariello, chef and owner of Savor Fresh Foods.

Consult chapter 10 for helpful information on such things as freezing tips and food-measurement equivalents.

Are you ready to cook? Or at least ready to *think* about getting ready to cook? Here are some tips to streamline the process.

First, read this introductory material. Then choose which menu cycle you would like to try this month and read through that chapter so you'll know what's ahead.

Next comes the hardest part: mark off the time on your calendar to grocery shop and cook! These should be on adjacent days. Don't try to shop and cook on the same day, especially if you have young children, or you won't like us very much! You simply won't have the time or energy to do both. You might also not like us about four hours into your cooking day, when your feet are complaining and every pot and pan you own is dirty. But we are consoled by the thought that you will like us *very much* when you peek at your larder, carefully labeled and layered in your freezer, as well as each day thereafter at about 5:00 P.M. The one-month cycles require about a nine-hour day (of course this varies with the cook). The two-week cycles take about five hours.

Cook with a friend or your spouse or an older child. The day goes so much more quickly when you divide the work and add conversation. If you have young children, a cooking companion can help tend the kids, answer the phone, and wipe the counters. You can either divide the food between your two families or cook one day a month at your friend's home and one day a month at your own.

Trust us that you will want to go out to dinner on cooking day! Yes, we know you will have plenty on hand for dinner. But you won't want to face any of it on your plate. This will pass. Go out, then have your spouse and kids wash the pots and pans.

Err on the side of buying a little more produce, chicken, and ground beef than is called for on your shopping lists. You can always use these for salads, soups, and sandwiches. If you have chicken broth left over, freeze it in an ice cube tray. When the cubes are frozen, pop them into a freezer bag. You can pull out a cube when a recipe calls for chicken broth, or make spur-of-the-moment chicken soup with leftovers.

You may want to photocopy the recipes and attach them to large index cards. In many cases you will be working on more than one recipe at a time. You can lay out your recipe cards in sequence to save you from having to keep turning the pages.

Don't even think about trying to do extra baking on your cooking day. If you enjoy making pie crust and want to use your own rather than a store-bought one, prepare the pie crust a couple of days ahead.

Finally, although you need to free yourself of commitments on your cooking day, the day will go much more easily if you feel free to take a break to tend to the children's needs, make a phone call, or just sit down to rest! Wear shoes that give your feet good support. Listen to your favorite music. Crack open a kitchen window for ventilation and to let the good smells pour out.

The secret of the method involves *doing all similar processes at once*: browning ground beef and chopping onions and cooking chicken only once rather than several times a month. Imagine the hours this saves!

Grocery Shopping Hints

Before you go to the supermarket or warehouse store, read the grocery and staples lists for the menu cycle you plan to use. The staples list contains items you need but probably have on hand. Look through your cupboards and add any missing staple items to the grocery shopping list. Also check the list of suggested freezer containers to see if you need to buy any of them.

For added convenience, photocopy the grocery list that we provide, then write in the other staple items or containers you'll need to buy. The grocery lists have been categorized by sections of food to help speed you through the store.

If you shop for a one-month menu cycle, you will have to push one cart and pull another. You may need to budget more carefully in order to set aside the funds needed to purchase food for all your dinner entrées at once. But keep in mind that over the course of the month you will save money on your food bill by cooking this way, since you'll be buying in bulk, eating out less often, and eliminating unplanned trips to the supermarket.

Your shopping trip will take you a couple of hours, so don't try to wedge it between two appointments. If you take young children, be sure to go when everyone is well fed and rested. It also helps to break up the trip. For example, go at midmorning to a discount food store to buy in bulk, have lunch at a favorite spot, and then finish any leftover shopping at the supermarket. Since this will be a lengthy shopping trip, plan your route through the supermarket so you visit the meat and dairy aisles last. If a friend or relative can baby-sit for you on shopping day, you will accomplish more in less time.

When you get home from shopping, you don't have to put everything away. Stack the canned goods and dry ingredients on a table or counter because you'll be using them soon. Keeping them within sight can inspire you for the task ahead!

The grocery shopping lists include some items with asterisks (*). These can be stored, because you will not need them until the day you serve the corresponding entrée. Mark the labels of these items to remind you not to use them by mistake.

The Day Before Cooking Day

After you've returned from the grocery store, clear off the kitchen counters, removing any appliances you won't be using. Create as much free countertop space as you can. Then, following the "Equipment Needed for Cooking Day" list, pull out your food processor, mixer, bowls—the tools you will need. If you have room, you may also want to get out the staple items.

Make sure you have all needed groceries on hand. Then perform the tasks that your chosen menu cycle outlines for "The Day Before Cooking Day."

If you don't have a food processor to chop and slice the vegetables, you may want to cut them up the day before cooking, since this is one of the most time-consuming tasks. Then store these vegetables (except mushrooms) in the refrigerator in cold water inside tightly sealed plastic containers. Or omit the water and seal them in zip-closure bags.

Finally, check the list of freezer containers needed for the entrées in your menu cycle and get out the ones you'll need. You can usually store entrées in freezer bags, unless they are layered (like lasagna) or contain a lot of liquid. Food stored in freezer bags can be thawed in the bag and then warmed in a suitable container.

Cooking Day

The assembly order for each menu cycle is a step-by-step guide to preparing all your entrees. Read through the assembly order before you start to cook. Since you will usually be working on more than one recipe at a time, getting an overview will give you a sense of how the steps flow together.

The following suggestions will help make this method work best for you:

Place an empty trash can in the center of the kitchen, and corral the pets where they won't be underfoot. You'll want to avoid wasted motion wherever possible on cooking day.

Use a timer—or two timers—to remind you something is in the oven or boiling for a certain length of time.

Pause to wash pots and pans as necessary. Washing dishes and wiping up periodically as you work will help you work more efficiently and make end-of-the-day cleanup easier.

If you sauté several food items in succession, use the same skillet. Sometimes you'll only need to wipe it out and put in the next ingredients. Put a Crock-Pot to work by using it overnight for brisket, for example, and then for soup or stew on cooking day.

Set frequently used spices in a row at the back of your work area. Use one set of measuring cups and spoons for wet ingredients and another for dry. That way you'll need to wash them less often.

You will *perform all similar tasks at once*. For example, do all the grating, chopping, and slicing of the carrots, celery, cheese, and onions. Set them aside in separate bowls or plastic bags. Cook all the chicken if you didn't do that the day before. Brown all the ground beef and sauté all the onions at one time. These tasks may seem tedious, but you will have accomplished a lot when you're finished, and assembling the dishes will go much faster.

At the close of your cooking day, save leftover sliced or diced vegetables and cooked meat for a soup, a salad, or for snacks.

Food Storage and Freezer Tips

As you complete recipes, set them aside on a table to cool. When two or three have cooled, label each with the name of the entrée, the date you prepared it, and reheating instructions so you won't have to consult the recipe when you are preparing to serve it. For example:

Aztec Quiche
10/08
Bake uncov. 40–50 mins. at 325°F

If a recipe calls for cheese to be sprinkled on top the last few minutes of baking, seal the grated cheese in a small freezer bag. Then tape the bag to the side or top of the corresponding entrée's container so that you are freezing the two together.

Make the best use of your 13 × 11 × 2-inch baking dishes. Spray a dish with non-stick spray, line the dish with heavy aluminum foil, seal the entrée, and freeze it. When the entrée has frozen completely, remove it in the foil and return it to the freezer.

When sealing food for freezing, remove as much air from the container as possible and seal it airtight. This will help guard against the cardboardlike taste called freezer burn. When using freezer bags, label the bag with an indelible marker before you insert the food.

Post the menu of foods you've prepared on your freezer or inside a cupboard door to help you choose each day's dinner and to keep an inventory of what entrées you've used. Check off the dishes as you serve them. For the freshest taste, seal containers airtight and use them within a month to six weeks. (For additional freezer storage tips, see chapter 10.)

Serving Suggestions

Remember each evening to pull the next night's entrée from the freezer and put it in the refrigerator to thaw. If the food is in a freezer bag, set the bag in a casserole dish to thaw, in case any liquid leaks out. You can also thaw the dish in the microwave the next day. Use the rule of thumb that by 9:00 A.M. you'll have decided what you'll serve for dinner that night.

Each recipe includes suggestions for salads or vegetables you might serve with the entrées. You'll find some of those recipes in chapter 8. Now that you've saved time on your entrées, try some new salads, vegetables, or desserts, whether you have company or the same familiar faces around your table.

You'll spend less time in the kitchen during the coming weeks. You will save time, money, and energy that you can invest in many other ways. Imagine how good it will feel to have entrées on hand, and to have an immediate answer to each day's nagging question "What's for dinner?"

Let's get cooking!

Equipment Needed for Cooking Day

On cooking day, you'll want to reuse bowls and pans as much as possible to conserve counter and stovetop space. The following equipment will be needed for most cooking cycles.

APPLIANCES

    blender or hand mixer
    Crock-Pot
    food processor or grater

POTS, PANS, AND SKILLETS

    1 extra-large pot, canning kettle, or 2 large pots
    1 large saucepan with lid
    1 medium saucepan with lid
    1 small saucepan
    1 large skillet
    1 medium skillet
    1 or 2 rimmed baking sheets

BOWLS AND CONTAINERS

    1 set of large, medium, and small mixing bowls
    8 to 12 small-to-medium bowls or plastic bags (for grated, sliced, or chopped ingredients)
    heavy-duty aluminum foil
    freezer bags—both gallon and quart bags

MISCELLANEOUS TOOLS

    can opener
    colander
    cutting board
    hot pads (oven mitts)
    kitchen scissors
    knives (cutting and paring)
    ladle
    2 sets measuring cups (one for wet ingredients and one for dry)
    2 sets measuring spoons
    metal or plastic serving spatula
    mixing spoons

MISCELLANEOUS TOOLS (*continued*)

  rolling pin
  rubber gloves (for deboning chicken and mixing food with your hands)
  rubber spatula
  tongs
  vegetable peeler
  wire whisk

2

Two-Week Entrée Plan A

Grocery Shopping and Staples Lists

An asterisk (*) after an item indicates it can be stored until you cook the dish with which it will be served. For example, the spaghetti will not be cooked until the day you serve Spaghetti. Mark those items with an "X" as a reminder that you will need them for an entrée.

When entrées require perishable foods to be refrigerated until served, you may want to use those dishes right away or buy the food the week you plan to serve the dish. For example, fresh mushrooms would spoil by the end of a month.

For the two-week entrée plan, you will need these food items as well as the ones in the staples list that follows:

GROCERY SHOPPING LIST

CANNED GOODS

1 12-ounce can tomato paste

4 28-ounce cans Italian-style or plain crushed tomatoes in puree

1 14.5-ounce can diced tomatoes

1 15-ounce can black beans

1 15-ounce can Stagg fat-free chili (or favorite brand)

1 4-ounce can mushroom stems and pieces

3 14.5-ounce cans beef broth

3 14.5-ounce cans fat-free chicken or vegetable broth

1 14.5-ounce can sauerkraut

1 15.25-ounce can whole kernel corn

1 16-ounce can whole berry cranberry sauce*

1 11-ounce can mandarin oranges*

1 16-ounce jar mild, chunky salsa

GRAINS, NOODLES, AND RICE

1 16-ounce package spaghetti*

4 hamburger buns*

1 16-ounce package regular white rice

15-ounce package Italian seasoned dry bread crumbs

1 1.25-ounce package taco seasoning mix

1 1.25-ounce envelope dried onion soup*

2 12-ounce packages wide egg noodles

1 12-ounce bag tortilla chips*

DAIRY PRODUCTS

3 large eggs

1 pint half-and-half

8 ounces plain yogurt

1 stick sweet, unsalted butter (4 ounces)

12 ounces sour cream

4 ounces feta cheese

2 ounces Swiss cheese, grated

6 ounces Monterey Jack cheese, grated

4 ounces mozzarella cheese, grated

MEAT, POULTRY, AND SEAFOOD

　　1 pound bulk Italian sausage
　　$\frac{1}{2}$ pound cooked kielbasa sausage
　　$\frac{1}{2}$ pound cooked ham
　　$3\frac{1}{2}$ pounds lean ground beef
　　real bacon bits
　　2 pounds thick boneless pork chops
　　$2\frac{1}{2}$ pounds beef roast
　　$1\frac{1}{2}$ pounds cooked, frozen small or medium shrimp
　　$1\frac{1}{2}$ pounds frozen tilapia fillets*
　　1 1.5-to-2-ounce flank steak
　　12 boneless, skinless chicken breasts
　　6 pounds boneless, skinless chicken pieces (breasts and/or thighs)

PRODUCE

　　5 medium onions
　　2 large carrots
　　1 green bell pepper
　　1 red bell pepper
　　2 bunches green onions
　　1 bunch fresh parsley
　　1 4.5-ounce jar crushed garlic
　　1 bunch celery
　　1 lemon
　　4 potatoes*
　　2 apples*

Make sure you have the following staples on hand; add those you don't have to your shopping list.

STAPLES LIST

　　bay leaves
　　Cajun seasoning
　　chili powder
　　black pepper
　　dry mustard
　　salt
　　sugar
　　curry powder

thyme, dried

basil leaves, dried

oregano, dried

catsup

Worcestershire sauce

paprika

soy sauce

sesame seeds

caraway seeds

red pepper flakes

ginger

honey (1 cup)

olive oil (2 tablespoons)

vegetable oil ($\frac{3}{4}$ cup)

red wine vinegar ($\frac{1}{4}$ cup)

Parmesan cheese, grated

Tabasco sauce

waxed paper

slivered almonds*

raisins*

shredded sweetened coconut*

Freezer Containers

The following is the list of freezer containers that will be needed for the entrées in this two-week cycle. They're not the only containers in which you could freeze these foods, but the list gives you an idea of the sizes and number of containers you'll need. Labeling containers before you cook works best.

6-cup container: Spaghetti

2-cup container: Baked Fish in Spaghetti Sauce

14-cup container: Taco Soup

$8\frac{1}{2} \times 12$-inch casserole dish: Stuffed Pork Chops

Heavy-duty aluminum foil: Stuffed Pork Chops

Waxed paper: Chili Hamburgers

Two-Week Entrée Plan A

SUN.	MON.	TUES.	WED.	THURS.	FRI.	SAT.
	1 Eat Out Cooking Day!	*2* Baked Jambalaya	*3* Stuffed Pork Chops	*4* Beef Goulash	*5* Caraway Pot Roast	*6* Spaghetti
7 Taco Soup	*8* Marinated Flank Steak	*9* Cranberry Chicken	*10* Twelve-Boy Curry	*11* Sweet Soy Marinated Chicken	*12* Chili Hamburgers	*13* Karen's Barbecued Chicken
14 Baked Fish in Spaghetti Sauce	*15* Fiesta Shrimp Dinner	*16*	*17*	*18*	*19*	*20*
21	*22*	*23*	*24*	*25*	*26*	*27*
28	*29*	*30*				

11 One-gallon freezer bags: Baked Fish in Spaghetti Sauce (1); Baked Jambalaya (1); Twelve-Boy Curry (1); Cranberry Chicken (1); Sweet Soy Marinated Chicken (1); Karen's Barbecued Chicken (1); Chili Hamburgers (1); Beef Goulash (1); Caraway Pot Roast (1); Marinated Flank Steak (1); Fiesta Shrimp Dinner (1)

The Day Before Cooking Day

1. Store those items you've purchased that will not be used until the dish is eaten (marked in each recipe by an asterisk [*]).
2. Set out appliances, bowls, canned goods, dry ingredients, freezer containers, and recipes.

On Cooking Day, Before Assembling Dishes

1. Make sure you've cleared the table and counters of unnecessary kitchenware to allow plenty of working room. It also helps to have fresh, damp washcloths and towels for wiping your hands and the cooking area. The day will go smoother if you clean and organize as you work.
2. Before you prepare a recipe, gather all the spices and ingredients in the assembly area to save time and steps. When you finish the recipe, remove unneeded items, and wipe off the work space.
3. Slightly undercook regular rice and noodles (al dente) that will be frozen. When you reheat them, they will have a better consistency and won't turn mushy.
4. Perform all chopping and slicing tasks.
    carrots: peel and slice 2
    green bell pepper: chop 1
    red bell pepper: chop 1
    fresh parsley: chop 1 cup
    green onions: chop 2 bunches
    celery: chop $1\frac{1}{2}$ cups
    onions: finely chop 5 medium
    kielbasa: slice $\frac{1}{2}$ pound
    ham: dice $\frac{1}{2}$ pound
    slice flank steak into $\frac{1}{2}$-inch strips against the grain
    cut 6 chicken breasts into strips
5. Treat the casserole dish you'll use with nonstick spray.

Assembly Order

As you assemble each group of the following entrées, allow them to cool if necessary, put them in storage containers, label them, and freeze.

ASSEMBLE PORK DISHES

1. Prepare Spaghetti Sauce. When spaghetti sauce has simmered for an hour, cool and freeze in the containers indicated. You will be freezing ingredients for Spaghetti, and Baked Fish in Spaghetti Sauce.
2. While Spaghetti Sauce simmers, combine ingredients for Baked Jambalaya and freeze.
3. Prepare Stuffed Pork Chops and freeze.

ASSEMBLE CHICKEN DISHES

1. Prepare Twelve-Boy Curry and freeze.
2. Prepare Cranberry Chicken and freeze.
3. Prepare Sweet Soy Marinated Chicken and freeze.
4. Prepare Karen's Barbecued Chicken and freeze.

ASSEMBLE BEEF DISHES

1. Prepare Chili Hamburgers and freeze.
2. While browning ingredients for Beef Goulash, prepare Caraway Pot Roast and freeze.
3. Prepare Taco Soup.
4. While Taco Soup boils, prepare Marinated Flank Steak and freeze.
5. Freeze Taco Soup.

ASSEMBLE SEAFOOD DISHES

1. Prepare Fiesta Shrimp Dinner and freeze.

Recipes for the Two-Week Entrée Plan A

Each recipe offers complete instructions on how to prepare the dish. Food items with an asterisk (*) won't be prepared until you serve the entrée. For recipes calling for oven baking, preheat oven for about 10 minutes.

The "summary of processes" gives a quick overview of foods that need to be chopped, diced, grated, or sliced. "Freeze in" tells what bags and containers will be needed to freeze each entrée. "Serve with" offers suggestions of foods to accompany the meal.

Some of the recipes for those foods are included in chapter 8.

Spaghetti Sauce

1 pound bulk Italian sausage
1½ cups finely chopped onion
1 12-ounce can tomato paste
3 28-ounce cans Italian-style or plain crushed tomatoes in puree
2 cups water
4 teaspoons minced garlic
4 bay leaves
2 tablespoons sugar
4 teaspoons dried basil leaves
2 teaspoons dried oregano leaves
4 tablespoons chopped fresh parsley
2 teaspoons salt
1 16-ounce package spaghetti*

In a large pot, cook and stir the bulk Italian sausage with onion until the meat is brown, about 15 minutes. Drain the fat. Add remaining ingredients, except the spaghetti. Bring sauce to a boil; reduce heat. Partly cover and simmer for 1 hour, stirring occasionally.

After sauce has cooled, freeze the sauce in the containers indicated below.

To prepare for serving spaghetti, thaw sauce and heat in a medium saucepan. Cook noodles according to package directions, drain, and pour sauce over them.

SUMMARY OF PROCESSES:
Chop 1½ cups onion and 4 tablespoons parsley.

FREEZE IN: 9-cup container for spaghetti; 2-cup container for Baked Fish in Spaghetti Sauce
SERVE WITH: Asparagus Italian

Makes 8 servings

Baked Fish in Spaghetti Sauce

$1\frac{1}{2}$ pounds frozen tilapia fillets*
 2 cups spaghetti sauce

Freeze 2 cups spaghetti sauce. Put the frozen tilapia fillets in a freezer bag and freeze.

When both are thawed, pour $\frac{3}{4}$ cup spaghetti sauce on bottom of baking dish, add fish, and cover fish with remaining spaghetti sauce. Bake at 350°F for 20 minutes or until flaky.

FREEZE IN: 1-gallon freezer bag; 1 2-cup container
SERVE WITH: Broiled Tomatoes

Makes 4 servings

Baked Jambalaya

3 tablespoons real bacon bits
$\frac{1}{2}$ cup chopped celery
$\frac{1}{2}$ cup chopped green bell pepper
2 tablespoons green onions, chopped
$\frac{1}{2}$ pound cooked kielbasa, sliced
$\frac{1}{2}$ pound diced cooked ham
$\frac{1}{2}$ teaspoon dried thyme
1 teaspoon Cajun seasoning
1 28-ounce can crushed tomatoes
1 14.5-ounce can beef broth
$1\frac{1}{2}$ cups uncooked regular long-grain white rice*

Mix together in a large mixing bowl all ingredients except rice. Pour into freezer bag, label and freeze.

Thaw, add rice, and put into greased 9 × 13-inch baking dish. Cover and bake at 375°F for 1 hour or until rice is done. Uncover and stir before serving.

SUMMARY OF PROCESSES:
Slice kielbasa and dice ham. Chop $\frac{1}{2}$ cup celery, $\frac{1}{2}$ cup green bell pepper, and 3 green onions.

FREEZE IN: 1-gallon bag
SERVE WITH: Black Bean, Collard Greens, and Spinach Salad

Makes 8 to 10 servings

Stuffed Pork Chops

2 pounds thick boneless pork chops (about 3)
1 cup grated mozzarella cheese
1 4-ounce can sliced mushroom stems and pieces
$\frac{1}{4}$ cup minced fresh parsley
$\frac{1}{2}$ teaspoon salt
$\frac{1}{4}$ teaspoon pepper
$\frac{1}{2}$ cup seasoned bread crumbs
1 large egg

In a small bowl combine cheese, mushrooms, parsley, salt and pepper. Take two pie pans and beat the egg in one; sprinkle the bread crumbs in the other.

Slit each pork chop lengthwise about $\frac{3}{4}$ of the way through the chop. Stuff with the cheese-mushroom mixture. Then dip and roll the chops first in the egg and then in the bread crumbs. Seal in a casserole dish treated with nonstick spray and freeze.

When thawed, add $\frac{1}{3}$ cup water to the casserole dish and cover with foil. Bake at 350°F for 40 minutes.

FREEZE IN: $8\frac{1}{2} \times 12$-inch casserole dish
SERVE WITH: Broiled Tomatoes

Makes 5 servings

Twelve-Boy Curry

6 boneless, skinless chicken breasts cut into strips
6 tablespoons sweet butter, divided
1 cup finely chopped onions
1 cup chopped celery
2 to 3 teaspoons crushed garlic
1 to 2 tablespoons curry powder
1 teaspoon dry mustard
$1\frac{1}{2}$ teaspoon salt
$\frac{1}{2}$ teaspoon pepper
1 teaspoon paprika
$1\frac{1}{2}$ cups beef broth
1 cup half-and-half
3 tablespoons catsup
Rice*
Shredded, sweetened coconut* (optional)
Raisins* (optional)
Chopped green onions* (optional)
Slivered almonds* (optional)
Mandarin oranges* (optional)

Cut chicken breasts into strips. In a large skillet, sauté chicken strips in 3 tablespoons butter until just cooked but not dry. Remove and melt another 3 tablespoons butter in the skillet. Add onion, celery, and garlic and sauté on medium heat until limp but not brown.

Combine dry ingredients and add to vegetable mixture. Stir until blended. Add remaining ingredients and cook slightly, stirring until well blended. Add cooked chicken and stir. Cool and freeze.

When thawed, heat through but do not overcook. Serve on rice. Good with condiments such as shredded, sweetened coconut, raisins, chopped green onions (using the whole onion), slivered almonds, and mandarin oranges.

SUMMARY OF PROCESSES:
Cut chicken into strips; finely chop 1 cup onions; chop 1 cup celery.

FREEZE IN: 1-gallon freezer bag
SERVE WITH: Gingered Carrots

Makes 6 to 8 servings

Cranberry Chicken

  6 boneless, skinless chicken breast halves
  2 envelopes dried onion soup*
  1 16-ounce can whole berry cranberry sauce*

Freeze chicken breasts in bag. When thawed, place chicken in greased baking pan, mix dry soup mix and cranberry sauce and spread over top. Cover with foil. Bake 40 minutes at 350°F or until done. Bake last 15 minutes uncovered. The whole house will smell wonderful.

  FREEZE IN: 1-gallon freezer bag
  SERVE WITH: Twice-Baked Sweet Potatoes

Makes 6 servings

Sweet Soy Marinated Chicken

  $2\frac{1}{2}$ pounds boneless, skinless chicken pieces (breasts and/or thighs)

MARINADE
  1 cup honey
  $\frac{3}{4}$ cup soy sauce
  2 tablespoons crushed garlic
  1 teaspoon ground ginger

Warm marinade ingredients together in microwave until honey is melted, about $1\frac{1}{2}$ minutes. Pour over chicken in freezer bag, label and freeze. When thawed, pour into baking dish, cover with foil, and bake for 30 minutes at 350°F. Uncover, turn chicken, and bake an additional 30 minutes.

  FREEZE IN: 1-gallon freezer bag
  SERVE WITH: Rice; Steamed Edamame

Makes 4 servings

Karen's Barbecued Chicken

$3\frac{1}{2}$ pounds boneless chicken pieces (breasts and/or thighs)
$\frac{3}{4}$ cup vegetable oil
$\frac{1}{3}$ cup soy sauce
3 tablespoons Worcestershire sauce
$\frac{1}{4}$ cup red wine vinegar
Juice of 1 lemon
1 tablespoon dry mustard
1 teaspoon salt
2 tablespoons minced fresh parsley
$\frac{1}{2}$ teaspoon crushed garlic

In a freezer bag combine all ingredients (spices together first, then add liquids, then chicken). Freeze.

When thawed, remove chicken, reserving marinade. Grill over medium hot coals 15 to 20 minutes, basting frequently with reserved marinade.

SUMMARY OF PROCESSES:

Mince 2 tablespoons fresh parsley.

FREEZE IN: 1-gallon freezer bag
SERVE WITH: Grilled mixed vegetables

Makes 5 servings

Chili Hamburgers

$1\frac{1}{2}$ pounds lean ground beef
3 tablespoons finely chopped green bell pepper
$\frac{1}{4}$ cup finely chopped onion
$1\frac{1}{2}$ tablespoon chili powder
2 dashes Tabasco sauce
$\frac{1}{2}$ teaspoon black pepper
1 teaspoon salt
4 hamburger buns*

Thoroughly mix all ingredients except hamburger buns. Shape into 4 hamburger patties. Wrap each in waxed paper and freeze in a large freezer bag, with waxed paper in between.

To prepare for serving, thaw patties and hamburger buns. Grill or fry patties to desired pinkness in center. Serve on warmed hamburger buns.

SUMMARY OF PROCESSES:
Finely chop 3 tablespoons green bell pepper and $\frac{1}{4}$ cup onion.

FREEZE IN: 1-gallon freezer bag, separated with waxed paper
SERVE WITH: Cauliflower Mock Potato Salad

Makes 4 large servings

Beef Goulash

2 pounds extra-lean ground beef

2 cups chopped onion

1 cup chopped red bell pepper (about one medium)

1 cup sliced carrots

1 teaspoon crushed garlic

$\frac{1}{3}$ cup catsup

1 tablespoon Worcestershire sauce

2 dashes Tabasco sauce

1 14.5-ounce can beef broth

2 teaspoons paprika

1 teaspoon salt

4 medium potatoes*

Brown the ground beef, chopped onion, and red pepper in a large skillet on medium heat. Drain and cool. Mix all ingredients together and place in one-gallon Ziploc bag. Label and freeze.

Thaw and put into a Crock-Pot. Add 4 potatoes peeled and cut. Make sure the potatoes are under the liquid. Cover and cook on low for 4 to 6 hours.

SUMMARY OF PROCESSES:

Chop 2 cups onion and 1 cup red bell pepper; slice 1 cup carrots.

FREEZE IN: 1-gallon freezer bag
SERVE WITH: Italian Parsley Salad

Makes 4 servings

Caraway Pot Roast

  1 large onion, chopped
  1 teaspoon crushed garlic
$2\frac{1}{2}$ pound roast beef, fat trimmed
  1 1-pound can sauerkraut, drained
  1 teaspoon caraway seeds
$\frac{1}{2}$ teaspoon salt
$\frac{1}{4}$ teaspoon pepper
  1 cup water
  2 apples (grate when served)*
  8 ounces wide egg noodles*

Place all ingredients except water, apples, and noodles in bag and seal well. Freeze. Thaw and put into Crock-Pot. Add water, cover, and turn on low for 6 to 8 hours. Shred the meat in the sauce to serve.

Chop two apples and put on top of sauce and meat. Serve on cooked noodles.

SUMMARY OF PROCESSES:

Chop $1\frac{1}{4}$ cup onion.

FREEZE IN: 1-gallon freezer bag
SERVE WITH: Green beans

Makes 5 to 6 servings

Taco Soup

3 14.5-ounce cans fat-free chicken or vegetable broth
1 14.5-ounce can diced tomatoes
1 15-ounce can black beans, drained
1 15-ounce can Stagg fat free chili (or favorite brand)
1 bunch chopped green onions
1 14.5-ounce can whole kernel corn
1 1.25-ounce package taco seasoning mix
Shredded Monterey Jack cheese*
Sour cream*
1 12-ounce bag tortilla chips*

Pour all ingredients except last 3 into a large pot and bring to a boil. Reduce heat and simmer for 10 minutes. Cool and pour into container to freeze.

When thawed, bring soup to a boil and simmer for 20 minutes.

SUMMARY OF PROCESSES:

Chop 1 bunch green onions.

FREEZE IN: 14-cup container
SERVE WITH: Jicama, cucumber, and orange salad

Makes 4 to 6 servings

Marinated Flank Steak

  1 1.5-to-2-pound flank steak cut into $\frac{1}{2}$-inch strips against the grain
  2 tablespoons sugar
  2 tablespoons soy sauce
12 tablespoons olive oil
  1 tablespoon sesame seeds
  $\frac{1}{2}$ teaspoon red pepper flakes, or to taste

Spread sesame seeds on pie pan and place in oven at 350°F for 5 minutes to toast them. Place all ingredients in bag and freeze. Before serving, thaw then pour contents of bag on a foil-lined rimmed baking sheet. Broil 4 to 5 minutes then turn meat and broil 2 to 3 minutes more or to desired doneness. Enjoy!

SUMMARY OF PROCESSES:

Cut 1 flank steak into $\frac{1}{2}$-inch strips against the grain.

FREEZE IN: 1-gallon freezer bag
SERVE WITH: Twice-Baked Sweet Potatoes; broccoli

Makes 4 servings

Fiesta Shrimp Dinner

    1½ pounds frozen cooked shrimp
    12 ounces wide egg noodles, cooked and drained
     4 ounces feta cheese
     ½ cup Swiss cheese
     ½ cup Monterey Jack cheese, shredded
    16 ounces mild, chunky salsa
     ¾ cup minced fresh parsley
     1 teaspoon dried basil
     1 teaspoon dried oregano
     2 large eggs
     1 cup half-and-half
     1 cup plain yogurt

Cook and drain noodles according to package directions. Drain and set aside to cool. Meanwhile, measure the three cheeses, salsa, parsley, and spices into medium bowl; add noodles and stir. In small bowl, mix well the eggs, half-and-half, and yogurt. Add to noodles. Label 1-gallon Ziploc bag. Tape frozen bag of shrimp to noodles, bag and freeze.

Thaw. Blot thawed, cooked shrimp with paper towel. Add shrimp to noodles and place in greased 9×13-inch prepared baking dish. Bake uncovered at 350°F for 25 to 30 minutes. Let stand 5 minutes before serving.

FREEZE IN: 1-gallon freezer bag
SERVE WITH: Hearts of Palm Salad; Vinaigrette

Makes 6 servings

3

Two-Week Entrée Plan B

Grocery Shopping and Staples Lists

As asterisk (*) after an item indicates that it should be stored until you cook the dish with which it will be served. For example, the corn tortillas and salsa will not be used until the day you serve Chile Verde. Mark those items with an "X" as a reminder that you will need them for an entrée.

When entrées require perishable foods to be refrigerated until served, you may want to prepare those dishes right away or buy the food the week you plan to make the dish. For example, fresh mushrooms would spoil by the end of a month.

For the low-fat entrée plan, you will need these food items as well as the ones in the staples list that follows.

GROCERY SHOPPING LIST

CANNED GOODS

   1 15.25-ounce can corn
   1 16-ounce can cut green beans
   1 8-ounce bottle lemon juice
   1 11-ounce can mandarin orange sections
   1 $10\frac{3}{4}$-ounce can cream of mushroom soup
   1 $10\frac{3}{4}$-ounce can cream of celery soup
   1 $10\frac{3}{4}$-ounce can cream of chicken soup
   1 46-ounce can Picante V8 juice
   1 6-ounce can tomato paste
   2 28-ounce can Italian-style or plain crushed tomatoes in puree
   1 4-ounce jar pimientos
   1 4-ounce can sliced ripe olives
   2 4-ounce mild diced chilies
   2 15-ounce cans pinto beans
   1 24-ounce jar salsa*
   $\frac{1}{4}$ cup French dressing

GRAINS, NOODLES, AND RICE

   1 16-ounce package regular rice
   8 Kaiser rolls*
   6 sandwich rolls*
   1 12-ounce package spaghetti
   1 16-ounce package wide egg noodles
   1 16-ounce package spinach or wide egg noodles
   1.25-ounce envelope dried onion soup
   1.15-ounce package au jus gravy mix
   1.15-ounce package brown gravy mix
   1 1.2-ounce packet dry spaghetti sauce seasoning
   1 32-ounce package long-grain rice
   1 dozen corn tortillas*

FROZEN FOODS

   $1\frac{1}{4}$ pounds frozen fish fillets (halibut, swordfish, or orange roughy)
   1 loaf frozen French bread dough
   1 6-ounce can frozen orange juice

DAIRY

　　　1 stick butter

　　　8 ounces low-fat sour cream

　　　3 tablespoons nonfat plain yogurt

　　　6 ounces sliced Monterey Jack cheese with jalapeños

　　　8 ounces Cheddar cheese, grated*

　　　4 ounces Monterey Jack cheese, grated*

MEAT AND POULTRY

　　　2 pounds chicken pieces

　　　5 pounds chicken breasts, boneless, skinless

　　　6 boneless, skinless chicken breasts, halved

　　　2 pounds beef round tip steak

　　　$1\frac{1}{2}$-pound London broil

　　　1 1-pound sirloin steak

　　　4 pounds extra-lean ground beef

　　　5 pounds pork loin

PRODUCE

　　　3 green bell peppers

　　　7 carrots

　　　1 4.5-ounce jar crushed garlic

　　　$1\frac{3}{4}$ pounds fresh mushrooms

　　　3 stalks celery

　　　1 bunch green onions

　　　$2\frac{1}{2}$ pounds white or yellow onions

　　　1 bunch fresh parsley

　　　6 white potatoes*

　　　5 or 6 new potatoes*

STAPLES LIST

　　Make sure you have the following staples on hand; add those you don't have to your shopping list.

　　　basil leaves, dried
　　　bay leaf
　　　beef bouillon cubes (2)
　　　catsup

Two-Week Entrée Plan B

SUN.	MON.	TUES.	WED.	THURS.	FRI.	SAT.
	1 Eat Out Cooking Day!	2 Hearty Hamburger-Tomato Stew	3 Chinese Chicken Morsels	4 Roast Beef Sandwiches with Au Jus	5 Grilled Fish	6 Chicken Spaghetti
7 Mandarin Orange Chicken	8 Grilled Chile Pepper Cheeseburgers	9 Rainy Day Chicken with Rice	10 Polynesian Pork Loin	11 Blackened Chicken Breast	12 Chicken Cacciatore	13 Meal-on-the-Run Pork Loin
14 Chile Verde	15 Savory Beef	16	17	18	19	20
21	22	23	24	25	26	27
28	29	30				

celery seeds

chicken bouillon cubes (6)

chili powder

cloves, ground

cumin, ground

Dijon mustard ($\frac{1}{4}$ cup)

dill weed

dry mustard

flour, all-purpose

garlic powder

garlic salt

ginger, ground

light brown sugar

light mayonnaise

low-fat margarine

nonstick spray

olive oil

onion powder

oregano leaves, dried

paprika

Parmesan cheese

pepper: cayenne, white, freshly ground black, and regular black

salt

soy sauce

sugar

thyme leaves, dried

vegetable oil (about $\frac{1}{2}$ cup)

white vinegar

Worcestershire sauce (3 tablespoons)

red wine ($\frac{1}{2}$ cup)

Freezer Containers

The following list of freezer containers or flat baking dishes will be needed for the entrées in the two-week cycle. They're not the only containers in which you could freeze
these foods, but the list gives you an idea of the size and number of containers you'll
need. Labeling containers before you cook works best.

1 empty spice jar or small container: Blackened Chicken

6 1-gallon freezer bags: Chinese Chicken Morsels (1); Roast Beef Sandwiches (1); Grilled Chile Pepper Cheeseburgers (1); Rainy Day Chicken w/Rice (1); Polynesian Pork Loin (1); Meal-on-the-Run Pork Loin (1)

5 1-quart freezer bags: Grilled Fish (1); Blackened Chicken (1); Chicken Spaghetti (1); Chile Verde (1); Rainy Day Chicken (1)

1 4-cup freezer container: Mandarin Orange Chicken

1 5-cup freezer container: Chile Verde

2 8-cup freezer containers: Savory Beef; Chicken Cacciatore

2 16-cup freezer containers: Hearty Hamburger Tomato Stew; Chicken Spaghetti

Waxed paper: Grilled Chile Pepper Cheeseburgers

The Day Before Cooking Day

1. Store those items you've purchased that will not be used until the dish is eaten (marked in each recipe by an asterisk*).
2. Set out appliances, bowls, canned goods, dry ingredients, freezer containers, and recipes.

On Cooking Day, Before Assembling Dishes

1. Put out a 6-ounce can of frozen orange juice concentrate to thaw.
2. Cook 2 pounds of ground beef until brown, about 15 minutes. Drain the oil and blot beef hash on a paper towel.
3. Cook $3\frac{1}{2}$ pounds of the boneless, skinless chicken breasts in a large casserole dish at 375°F for 50 minutes, covered. When cooled, cut the chicken into cubes.
4. Perform all chopping, grating, and slicing tasks.
   Green onions: Chop onion bulbs only, discard green tops.
   Carrots: Slice 7.
   Mushrooms: Slice all.
   Celery: Slice 3 stalks.
   Green bell peppers: Chop 2; slice half of the other into thin strips.
   Onions: Slice 2 onions; chop the rest.

Beef: Slice round tip steak into strips about 2 inches long.

Cut 6 boneless, skinless chicken breasts into long strips and 7 boneless, skinless chicken breasts into cubes (kitchen scissors work best) and refrigerate until needed.

5. Treat baking dishes and pie or pizza pans you will need with nonstick spray.
6. As you assemble each group of the following entrées, allow them to cool if necessary, put them in storage containers, and freeze.

Assembly Order

ASSEMBLE BEEF DISHES

1. Combine ingredients for Roast Beef Sandwiches and freeze.
2. Assemble and start cooking Chile Verde.
3. Complete Savory Beef in a skillet. Allow to cool, label and freeze.
4. Prepare Grilled Chile Pepper Cheeseburgers and freeze.
5. Mix ingredients for Hearty Hamburger Tomato Stew and start it simmering.
6. As soon as these dishes are completed and have cooled, label each one and freeze.

ASSEMBLE PORK DISHES

1. Make marinade for Grilled Fish.
2. Assemble and Meal-on-the-Run Pork Loin and freeze.
3. Prepare Polynesian Pork Loin.
4. Label and freeze these dishes.

ASSEMBLE CHICKEN DISHES

1. Make Rainy Day Chicken with Rice in one large skillet or pan with lid and Chicken Cacciatore in another.
2. While these are simmering, assemble Chinese Chicken Morsels.
3. Mix spices for Blackened Chicken Breasts.
4. Prepare Mandarin Orange Chicken.
5. Assemble Chicken Spaghetti, cooking noodles while chicken and tomato sauce are simmering.
6. Complete Chile Verde; allow to cool.
7. Label and freeze this last batch of dishes.

Take a minute to enjoy looking into your freezer at all the food you've prepared!

Recipes for the Two-Week Entrée Plan B

Each recipe offers complete instructions on how to prepare the dish. Food items with an asterisk (*) won't be prepared until you serve the entrée. For recipes calling for oven baking, preheat oven for about 10 minutes.

"Summary of processes" gives a quick overview of foods that need to be chopped, diced, grated, or sliced. "Freeze in" tells what bags and containers will be needed to freeze each entrée. "Serve with" offers suggestions of foods to accompany the meal. Some of the recipes for those foods are included in chapter 8. "Note" includes special instructions on how the entrée can be used in other ways.

Roast Beef Sandwiches Au Jus

1 1½-pound London broil
1.15-ounce package au jus gravy mix
1.15-ounce package brown gravy mix
3 cups water

Trim fat off meat. Sprinkle gravy mixes on London broil in 1-gallon Ziploc bag. Label and freeze. Thaw, add 3 cups water to bag and shake. Pour into Crock-Pot and cook (low) for 3 to 4 hours. Slice meat and return to sauce. Serve on toasted buns. Great for picnics.

> **FREEZE IN:** 1-gallon bag
> **SERVE WITH:** Corn on the Cob with Chili Butter
> **NOTE:** For variation, sour cream can be added to the cooked meat then served on noodles.

Makes 4 servings

Chile Verde

1   15-ounce can pinto beans, drained
1   pound boneless, skinless chicken breasts, cooked
1   4-ounce can chopped green chilies
1   teaspoon ground cumin
$\frac{3}{4}$ teaspoon dried oregano leaves
$\frac{1}{8}$ teaspoon cayenne pepper
3   cups water
3   chicken bouillon cubes
1   teaspoon minced garlic (1 clove)
1   teaspoon salt
$\frac{2}{3}$ cup finely chopped onion
1   cup grated Monterey Jack cheese*
1   dozen corn tortillas*
1   24-ounce jar salsa*

Combine chicken with chilies and seasonings; refrigerate until needed. At the same time, combine beans, water, bouillon cubes, garlic, salt, and onion in a large pot; bring to a boil.

Reduce heat and simmer until beans are soft, about 1 hour. Add more water if necessary.

Combine chicken and spices with beans; simmer 10 more minutes. Cool and freeze. Grate cheese, put it in a 1-quart bag and attach it to the freezer container with the chili.

To serve, thaw chili and cheese; serve on warmed corn tortillas.

SUMMARY OF PROCESSES:
Cut 1 pound boneless chicken into 1-inch cubes; chop $\frac{2}{3}$ cup onion.

FREEZE IN: 5-cup container; 1-quart bag
SERVE WITH: Fresh tomato and avocado slices

Makes 6 servings

Savory Beef

 2 pounds beef round tip steak
Freshly ground black pepper to taste
 1 cup sliced fresh mushrooms
 1 sliced onion
 3 tablespoons vegetable oil
 3 tablespoons all-purpose flour
 2 cups water
 2 beef bouillon cubes
 2 tablespoons tomato paste
 1 teaspoon dry mustard
 $\frac{1}{4}$ teaspoon dried oregano leaves
 $\frac{1}{4}$ teaspoon dill weed
 2 tablespoons Worcestershire sauce
8-ounces wide egg noodles*

Cut beef into thin strips about 2 inches long. Sprinkle beef with pepper and set meat aside in a cool place. In a heavy skillet, sauté mushrooms and onions in oil until golden, about 10 to 15 minutes. Remove them from skillet. Put meat in same skillet; cook and stir steak quickly on all sides until it's brown but still rare in the center, about 7 minutes. Remove meat and set aside.

Blend flour into the drippings in skillet, gradually adding water and beef bouillon. Bring to a boil. Stir constantly until smooth and slightly thick. Mix in tomato paste, dry mustard, oregano, dill weed, and Worcestershire sauce. Stir meat, mushrooms, and onions into sauce. Cool meat mixture and freeze.

To prepare for serving, thaw beef. Prepare noodles according to package directions. Heat beef in a saucepan over medium heat, stirring constantly until it's bubbly. Serve meat over noodles.

SUMMARY OF PROCESSES:
Slice 1 cup fresh mushrooms and 1 onion.

FREEZE IN: 8-cup container
SERVE WITH: Baked cauliflower; gingerbread
NOTE: Use any leftover beef for sandwiches

Makes 6 servings

Grilled Chile Pepper Cheeseburgers

$\frac{1}{3}$ cup finely chopped green onion

3 tablespoons nonfat plain yogurt

1 to 4 tablespoons seeded, finely chopped jalapeño peppers

$\frac{1}{2}$ teaspoon black pepper

$\frac{1}{2}$ teaspoon salt

2 pounds ground beef

6 ounces Monterey Jack cheese with jalapeño peppers, cut into 6 slices*

8 kaiser rolls, split and toasted*

In a medium bowl combine green onions, yogurt, jalapeño peppers, black pepper, and salt. Add beef and mix well. Shape mixture into 8 patties about $\frac{3}{4}$ inch thick. Freeze in a freezer bag with waxed paper placed between each patty. Grill the burgers until no pink remains in the center. Turn once. Top each patty with cheese the last 2 minutes of grilling time.

SUMMARY OF PROCESSES:

Finely chop $\frac{1}{3}$ cup green onion and 1–4 tablespoons jalapeño peppers.

FREEZE IN: 1-gallon bag

SERVE ON: Buns with lettuce and tomato. Pass chips and Steamed Edamame.

Makes 6 to 8 servings

Hearty Hamburger-Tomato Stew

    1 pound lean ground beef
 1¼ cups chopped onion
    2 cups peeled and sliced carrots
    1 cup chopped green bell pepper
    1 cup sliced fresh mushrooms
    1 16-ounce can cut green beans, drained
    1 16-ounce can corn, drained
    3 stalks sliced celery
    1 46-ounce can Picante V8 tomato juice
    2 teaspoons sugar
    1 teaspoon celery seeds
Salt and pepper to taste

Cook ground beef in a large saucepan until brown, about 10 to 15 minutes. Drain the fat and mix in remaining ingredients. Bring to a boil; reduce heat. Simmer covered 30 minutes, stirring occasionally. Cool and freeze.

To prepare for serving, thaw stew. Then bring to a boil; reduce heat; simmer 10 minutes.

SUMMARY OF PROCESSES:

Chop 1¼ cups onion and 1 cup green bell pepper; peel and slice 2 cups carrots, slice 1 cup fresh mushrooms, 3 stalks celery.

FREEZE IN: 16-cup container
SERVE WITH: Parsnip Fries

Makes 8 servings

Grilled Fish

$1\frac{1}{4}$ pounds frozen fish fillets (halibut, swordfish, or orange roughy)*
5 to 6 new potatoes* (bake with Thai fish sauce)

MARINADE

$\frac{1}{2}$ cup soy sauce
$\frac{1}{4}$ cup water
1 chicken bouillon cube
2 tablespoons olive oil
1 tablespoon light brown sugar
1 teaspoon crushed garlic
$\frac{1}{2}$ teaspoon ground ginger

Freeze fish fillets and store new potatoes until you're ready to serve them. Whisk remaining ingredients in a small bowl to make marinade. Freeze in a plastic bag taped to fish fillet package.

To prepare for serving, thaw marinade and fish fillets. Marinate fish 30 minutes.

At the same time, remove fish from the marinade. Set oven control to broil, or 550°F. Broil or grill fish for 10 minutes per inch of thickness or until fish flakes easily with a fork. Baste frequently with marinade while cooking. If fish is more than 1 inch thick, turn once during cooking.

FREEZE IN: 1-quart bag taped to fish fillet package
SERVE WITH: Baked new potatoes with Thai fish sauce; Sautéed Napa Cabbage

Makes 4 servings

Meal-on-the-Run Pork Loin

1   $3\frac{1}{2}$-pound pork loin
5   ounces soy sauce
$\frac{1}{4}$ cup light brown sugar
$\frac{1}{2}$ cup red cooking wine
1   tablespoon lemon juice
1   teaspoon Worcestershire sauce
$1\frac{1}{2}$ cups water

Trim fat off pork loin. Place all ingredients in bag and seal well. Freeze.

Thaw and place in Crock-Pot. Cover and set on low for 6 to 8 hours. If possible, turn several times to coat meat with sauce. When done, shred meat and return to sauce. NOTE: Good on hamburger buns for a picnic supper after a late soccer game.

FREEZE IN: 1-gallon bag
SERVE WITH: Crudités; Reese's Chewy Chocolate Cookies

Makes 6 to 8 servings

Polynesian Pork Loin

1 1$\frac{1}{2}$-pound pork loin
$\frac{1}{3}$ cup soy sauce
$\frac{1}{4}$ teaspoon ground ginger
$\frac{1}{2}$ teaspoon garlic powder

Cut 1$\frac{1}{2}$-pound pork loin into desired thickness. Place other ingredients in bag and add pork. Turn several times to cover meat with marinade. Label and freeze.

Thaw. Layer in prepared baking pan. Pour extra marinade over meat. Cover and cook in a preheated 350°F oven for 30 minutes. Turn and bake an additional 20 minutes.

FREEZE IN: 1-gallon bag

SERVE WITH: Yams. Wash yams, pierce several places with a fork, and wrap with foil. Place in oven and cook while meat is cooking. Yams should bake at least 60 minutes. When soft, remove foil and slit lengthwise. Squeeze ends together and fill with a mixture of butter, cinnamon, and brown sugar.

Makes 4 to 5 servings

Rainy Day Chicken with Rice

1 10¾-ounce can cream of mushroom soup
1 10¾-ounce can cream of celery soup
1 10¾-ounce can cream of chicken soup
¼ cup butter, melted
¼ cup French dressing
¼ cup milk
1½ cups long-grain uncooked rice
6 boneless, skinless chicken breasts cut into long strips
¼ cup grated Parmesan cheese

Mix together all but the Parmesan cheese and pour into freezer bag. Put Parmesan cheese in small bag and attach to chicken bag. Label and freeze.

When thawed, pour into 13×9-inch greased casserole dish and cover with foil. Bake at 350°F oven for 1½ hours. Add Parmesan cheese during the last 10 minutes of cooking.

SUMMARY OF PROCESSES:

Cut 6 boneless chicken breasts into long strips.

FREEZE IN: 1-gallon bag; 1-quart bag
SERVE WITH: 4 to 5 small zucchini sliced and sautéed in olive oil until tender but not limp. Fresh brownies would be a nice accompaniment to this cozy dinner.

Makes 8 servings

Chinese Chicken Morsels

1 pound boneless, skinless chicken breasts (2 cups)

MARINADE

$\frac{1}{2}$ cup lemon juice

$\frac{1}{4}$ cup soy sauce

$\frac{1}{4}$ cup Dijon mustard

2 teaspoons vegetable oil

$\frac{1}{4}$ teaspoon cayenne pepper

1 cup long-grain, uncooked rice*

Cut chicken breasts (kitchen scissors work best) into 1-inch cubes. Mix lemon juice, soy sauce, mustard, oil, and pepper. Put marinade and chicken cubes in a 1-gallon bag and store in the freezer.

To prepare for serving, thaw chicken and remove from marinade. Bring marinade to boil in a small saucepan. Place chicken cubes about an inch apart on broiler pan treated with nonstick spray. Broil 4 to 5 inches from heat for 7 minutes, brushing with marinade once. Turn chicken cubes and broil another 4 minutes. Meanwhile, prepare rice according to package directions.

SUMMARY OF PROCESSES:

Cut chicken into 1-inch cubes.

FREEZE IN: 1-gallon bag

SERVE WITH: Lentil Salad

NOTE: For a luncheon alternative, toss sautéed or broiled chicken morsels with mixed salad greens, shredded carrots, cherry tomatoes, chopped green bell pepper, sliced water chestnuts, and croutons. Use your favorite low-calorie dressing.

Makes 4 to 5 servings

Blackened Chicken Breasts

$1\frac{1}{2}$ pounds boneless, skinless chicken breasts*
6 sandwich rolls*
1 tablespoon vegetable oil*
Butter or mayonnaise*
$\frac{1}{4}$ cup melted butter* [later]

SPICE MIX*
2 teaspoons paprika
1 teaspoon onion powder
1 teaspoon garlic powder
$\frac{1}{4}$ teaspoon cayenne pepper
$\frac{1}{2}$ teaspoon white pepper
$\frac{1}{2}$ teaspoon black pepper
$\frac{1}{2}$ teaspoon salt
$\frac{1}{2}$ teaspoon dried thyme leaves
$\frac{1}{2}$ teaspoon dried oregano leaves

Freeze chicken and sandwich rolls until ready to serve. Mix spices; store in a covered container such as an empty spice jar, which you've labeled "Blackened Chicken Spices."

To serve, thaw rolls and chicken. Coat each piece of chicken with about 1 tablespoon spice mix. The mixture is hot and spicy, so adjust amount for taste of each person. Using a pastry brush, baste each piece of chicken with melted butter. Grill chicken, basting with butter again after turning once. Grill about 10 minutes or until no longer pink in the middle. Or cook chicken in a large, nonstick skillet in hot oil over medium heat. Cook, turning chicken once, until it's done, about 10 minutes. Serve on sandwich rolls spread with a little butter or light mayonnaise.

FREEZE IN: 1-quart bag; 1 small jar
SERVE WITH: Chips; Watermelon Salad
NOTE: Use spice mix on your favorite fish fillets.

Makes 6 servings

Mandarin Orange Chicken

1 pound boneless, skinless chicken breasts (2 cups), cooked and chopped
    into bite-size pieces
1 tablespoon vegetable oil
2 cups sliced, fresh mushrooms
2 teaspoons all-purpose flour
1 cup water
$\frac{1}{2}$ 6-ounce can frozen orange juice concentrate, thawed
$\frac{1}{2}$ cup thinly sliced green onion bulbs (without greens)
2 chicken bouillon cubes
1 11-ounce can mandarin orange sections, drained*
1 cup long-grain, uncooked rice*

In skillet, sauté mushrooms in oil over medium high heat, stirring constantly. Sprinkle flour over mushrooms, stirring quickly to combine. Gradually stir in water, orange juice concentrate, green onions, and bouillon cubes. Stirring constantly, bring to a boil. Reduce heat, add chicken, and let simmer 3 to 4 minutes. Cool and freeze.

To serve, thaw chicken mixture, and cook rice according to package directions. Heat chicken mixture in a saucepan until bubbly, stir in drained orange segments and heat through. Combine with cooked rice and serve.

SUMMARY OF PROCESSES:

Chop cooked chicken into bite-size pieces; slice 2 cups fresh mushrooms,
$\frac{1}{2}$ cup green onion bulbs.

FREEZE IN: 4-cup container
SERVE WITH: Apple-Spinach Salad

Makes 4 servings

Chicken Spaghetti

  1 16-ounce package spaghetti
 1½ pounds boneless, skinless chicken breasts (3 cups cooked)
  1 28-ounce can Italian-style or plain crushed tomatoes in puree
  2 ounces pimientos
  1 cup chopped green bell pepper
  1 cup chopped celery
  1 cup sliced fresh mushrooms
 1½ cups chopped onion
  1 4-ounce can sliced black ripe olives
  1 1.2-ounce packet dry spaghetti sauce seasoning
Salt and pepper to taste
  2 cups grated Cheddar cheese*

Cook spaghetti until al dente; drain. At the same time, cut chicken into 1-inch cubes; cook chicken in a small amount of water until no longer pink in the center, about 15 minutes. In a large pot, combine chicken with remaining ingredients except cheese. Bring mixture to a boil; reduce heat. Simmer for 15 minutes, stirring occasionally. Add cooked spaghetti to sauce. Cool and freeze in 16-cup container; tape 1-quart bag with cheese to container.

To prepare for serving, thaw cheese and spaghetti. Bake spaghetti in a preheated 325°F oven for 40 minutes. Top spaghetti with cheese; return spaghetti to oven for 5 minutes or until cheese melts.

SUMMARY OF PROCESSES:

 Cut 1½ pounds cooked chicken into 1-inch cubes; chop 1 cup green bell pepper, 1 cup celery, and 1½ cups onion; slice 1 cup fresh mushrooms.

 FREEZE IN: 16-cup container; 1-quart bag
 SERVE WITH: Baked asparagus

Makes 10 servings

Chicken Cacciatore

1 pound boneless, skinless chicken breasts (cut into 1-inch cubes)
1 tablespoon vegetable oil
1 sliced medium onion
$\frac{1}{2}$ sliced green bell pepper
2 cups fresh mushrooms
$\frac{1}{2}$ teaspoon crushed garlic
1 28-ounce can Italian-style or plain crushed tomatoes in puree
2 tablespoons chopped fresh parsley
1 teaspoon salt
$\frac{1}{4}$ teaspoon pepper
2 teaspoons Italian seasoning
1 teaspoon dried basil leaves
1 16-ounce package spinach or wide egg noodles (use half)*
$\frac{1}{2}$ cup grated Parmesan cheese*

Cut chicken into 1-inch cubes. In a large skillet, sauté chicken in vegetable oil until no longer pink in the center, about 15 minutes. Allow sauce to cool, put in an 8-cup container, cover and freeze.

To serve, thaw dish, and bake chicken in a preheated oven at 350°F for 35 minutes. Cook half package spinach or egg noodles according to directions. Serve chicken over noodles and sprinkle on Parmesan cheese.

SUMMARY OF PROCESSES:

Cut 1 pound chicken into cubes; slice 1 medium onion, $\frac{1}{2}$ green bell pepper, 2 cups fresh mushrooms.

FREEZE IN: 8-cup container
SERVE WITH: Hearts of Palm Salad

Makes 6 servings

4

Two-Week Entrée Plan C

Grocery Shopping and Staples Lists

An asterisk (*) after an item indicates it can be stored until you cook the dish with which it will be served. For example, the can of Mandarin oranges will not be needed until the day you serve Country Captain. Mark those items with an "X" before you put them away as a reminder that you will need them for an entrée.

When entrées require perishable foods to be refrigerated until served, you may want to use those dishes right away or buy the food the week you plan to prepare the dish.

For this two-week entrée plan you will need these food items as well as the ones on the staples list that follows. Note: See chapter 10 for equivalent measures.

GROCERY SHOPPING LIST

CANNED GOODS

      1 4-ounce can mushroom stems and pieces

      1 10$\frac{3}{4}$-ounce can cream of mushroom soup

      4 14$\frac{1}{2}$-ounce cans stewed tomatoes

      1 8-ounce can tomato sauce

      2 15-ounce cans tomato sauce

      1 26-ounce jar marinara sauce

      1 14$\frac{1}{2}$-ounce can diced tomatoes

      1 cup salsa, medium or mild

      4 15-ounce cans black beans

      2 4-ounce cans chopped green chilies

      1 12-ounce can evaporated milk or evaporated skim milk

      1 14$\frac{1}{2}$-ounce can diced tomatoes with green chilies

      1 4.5-ounce jar crushed garlic

GRAINS, PASTA, AND RICE

      2 5.7-ounce boxes of couscous* (or enough to serve 6)

      1 32-ounce bag of rice*

      2 8-ounce boxes lasagna

      1 8-ounce box linguine*

      6 whole wheat buns*

      12 ounces extra-thick egg noodles

DRY INGREDIENTS AND SEASONINGS

      Italian-style dry bread crumbs

      1 1.25-ounce package taco seasoning mix

      1 11-ounce bag of Fritos, or other corn chips*

      1 11-ounce bag tortilla chips*

      1$\frac{1}{2}$ tablespoons pure horseradish (spice)

      1 small package slivered almonds (optional)

FROZEN FOODS

      1 16-ounce-bag frozen corn

      1 30-ounce-bag frozen shredded hash brown potatoes

DAIRY PRODUCTS

1 stick sweet, unsalted butter (4 ounces)

grated Parmesan cheese ($\frac{3}{4}$ cup)

10 ounces grated Monterey Jack cheese

4 ounces Monterey Jack cheese with jalapeño peppers

6 ounces grated mozzarella cheese

2 ounces grated Swiss

12 ounces grated Cheddar cheese

5 large eggs

16 ounces ricotta cheese

2 cups milk

8 ounces cottage cheese

8 ounces light cream cheese

8 ounces plain low-fat yogurt

8 ounces sour cream*

MEAT, POULTRY, AND SEAFOOD

10 pounds boneless, skinless chicken breasts

5 pounds lean ground beef

1 $2\frac{1}{2}$-pound beef roast

2 pounds London broil

$\frac{1}{3}$ pound fully cooked ham

1 pound Italian sausage

1 pound smoked sausage links

PRODUCE

1 bunch green onions

$\frac{1}{4}$ cup currants or raisins

7 medium yellow onions

4 large baking potatoes*

8 new potatoes*

3 green bell peppers

1 bunch celery

1 bunch parsley

1 lemon

lettuce*

2 tomatoes*

2 avocados*

Two-Week Entrée Plan C

SUN.	MON.	TUES.	WED.	THURS.	FRI.	SAT.
	1 Eat Out Cooking Day!	2 Herbed Chicken	3 Winter Pot Roast	4 French Stuffed Potatoes	5 Chicken Nuggets	6 Playoff Burgers
7 Farmer's Casserole	8 Poppy Beef	9 Pizza in a Bowl	10 Country Captain	11 Denise's Black Beans	12 Chicken Taco Salad	13 London Broil
14 Mexican Chicken Lasagna	15 Sopa de Maiz	16	17	18	19	20
21	22	23	24	25	26	27
28	29	30				

barbecue sauce*
basil
bay leaves
black pepper
catsup (1 cup)
cayenne pepper
chicken bouillon cubes (4)
cornstarch
cumin
curry powder
fennel seeds
ginger, ground
light brown sugar
mace or nutmeg, ground
onion salt
oregano leaves, dried
poppy seeds
salt
steak sauce (A.1., et al.)
sugar
thyme leaves, dried
vegetable oil
Worcestershire sauce

Freezer Containers

The following list of freezer containers or flat baking dishes will be needed for the entrées in this two-week entrée plan. They're not the only containers in which you can freeze these foods, but the list gives you an idea of the size and number of containers you'll need. Labeling containers before you cook works best.

11 1-gallon freezer bags: Chicken Nuggets (1); Herbed Chicken (1); Country Captain (1); French Stuffed Potatoes (1); Poppy Beef (2); Winter Pot Roast (1); Playoff Burgers (1); Spaghetti Soup (1); London Broil (1); Chicken Taco Salad (1)

5   1-quart freezer bags: Chicken Nuggets (1); French Stuffed Potatoes (1); Spaghetti Soup (2); Chicken Taco Salad (1)

2   9×13×2-inch baking dishes: Mexican Chicken Lasagna; Farmer's Casserole

2   6-cup containers: Sopa de Maiz; Denise's Black Beans

The Day Before Cooking Day

1. Store all the items that you will not be using until the day you serve the dish. Be sure to label each so you won't forget and use them for other dishes.
2. Cook 4 pounds boneless, skinless chicken breasts in a large casserole dish in the oven, covered at 375°F for 50 minutes. Cool and cube the cooked chicken. Refrigerate until ready to use on cooking day.
3. Set out appliances, canned goods, dry ingredients, freezer containers, and recipes.

On Cooking Day, Before Assembling Dishes

1. Make sure you've cleared the table and counters of unnecessary kitchenware to allow plenty of working room. It also helps to have fresh, damp washcloths and towels for wiping your hands and the cooking area. The day will go a lot more smoothly if you clean and organize as you work.
2. Before you prepare a recipe, gather all the spices and ingredients in the assembly area to save time and steps. When you finish the recipe, remove unneeded items and wipe off the work space.
3. Perform all chopping, crushing, grating, and slicing tasks.
    Lemon zest: Grate 2 tablespoons.
    Celery: Slice $1\frac{1}{2}$ cups.
    Green pepper: Chop 3.
    Green onions: Slice $\frac{1}{4}$ cup.
    Onions: Chop 7.
    Ham: Cube $\frac{1}{3}$ pound.
    Smoked sausage: Slice 1 pound.
    Chicken: Cube 2 pounds raw chicken.
    Boneless chicken breast: Cube 3 pounds (use kitchen scissors for the best results).

Assembly Order

ASSEMBLE CHICKEN DISHES

1. Assemble Chicken Taco Salad.
2. Assemble Mexican Chicken Lasagna.
3. Assemble Sopa de Maiz.
4. Assemble Chicken Nuggets.
5. Assemble Herbed Chicken.
6. Assemble Country Captain.
7. Label and freeze chicken dishes.

ASSEMBLE BEEF DISHES

1. Assemble Denise's Black Beans in a Crock-Pot
2. Assemble Winter Pot Roast.
3. Assemble Poppy Beef.
4. Assemble Playoff Burgers.
5. Make sauce for London Broil.
6. Assemble French Stuffed Potatoes.
7. Label and freeze beef dishes.

ASSEMBLE SEAFOOD AND MISCELLANEOUS DISHES

1. Assemble Spaghetti Soup.
2. Assemble Farmer's Casserole.
3. Label and freeze these two dishes.
4. Cool Denise's Black Beans after they've cooked for 8 hours. Label and freeze.

Recipes for the Two-Week Entrée Plan C

Each recipe offers complete instructions on how to prepare the dish. Food items with an asterisk (*) won't be prepared until you serve the entrée. For recipes calling for oven baking, preheat oven for about 10 minutes.

"Summary of processes" gives a quick overview of foods that need to be chopped, diced, grated, or sliced. "Freeze in" tells what bags and containers will be needed to freeze each entrée. "Serve with" offers suggestions of foods to accompany the meal. Some of the recipes for those foods are included in chapter 8. "Note" includes special instructions on how the entrée can be used in other ways.

Chicken Taco Salad

   4 boneless, skinless chicken breasts, cooked and chopped
   1 14½-ounce can diced tomatoes with green chilies
   1 1¼-ounce packet taco seasoning
   1 cup grated Cheddar cheese*
Iceberg lettuce*
   2 tomatoes*
   1 avocado*
   1 11-ounce bag tortilla chips*

Pour first three ingredients in a gallon freezer bag. Measure the grated Cheddar cheese into a small freezer bag and tape it to the bag for the chicken mixture. Freeze.

When thawed, place ingredients in a slow cooker. Cover and cook on low for 4 to 5 hours. Cut up chicken and return to sauce. Make salad with finely chopped head lettuce, tomatoes, shredded Cheddar cheese, diced avocado, and tortilla chips. Toss in chicken mixture and serve. Great for a summer backyard meal.

FREEZE IN: 1-gallon bag; 1-quart bag
SERVE WITH: Brownies

Makes 6 servings

Mexican Chicken Lasagna

$\frac{3}{4}$ cup chopped onion

3 14-ounce cans stewed tomatoes with juice

$\frac{1}{2}$ cup salsa, medium or mild

1 1.25-ounce package taco seasoning

1 15-ounce can black beans, rinsed and drained

1 large egg

16 ounces ricotta cheese

1 teaspoons crushed garlic

10 ounces lasagna noodles

4 boneless, skinless cooked chicken breasts (about $1\frac{1}{2}$ pound) cooked and cut into 1-inch cubes

1 4-ounce can chopped green chilies

$1\frac{1}{2}$ cups (about 6 ounces) grated Monterey Jack cheese

To make sauce, combine chopped onion with tomatoes, salsa, and taco seasoning. Stir in beans.

To make ricotta layer, whisk egg in small bowl with a fork. Whisk in ricotta cheese and garlic.

Spread 1 cup tomato sauce mixture over the bottom of a greased 13×9×2-inch casserole dish (should barely cover bottom). Top with 5 (uncooked) noodles, overlapping slightly, then with half the chicken. Spread on one half of the ricotta cheese mixture; spread lightly. Sprinkle with half the grated cheese. Top with remaining noodles, chicken, chilies, tomato sauce mixture, and grated cheese. Cover with foil, label and freeze.

To prepare for serving, thaw and preheat oven to 350°F. Bake uncovered for 40 minutes, or until noodles are tender when pierced with sharp knife. Cool 10 minutes before serving.

SUMMARY OF PROCESSES:

Chop $\frac{3}{4}$ cup onion; cut 4 boneless, skinless cooked chicken breasts into 1-inch cubes.

FREEZE IN: 13×9×2-inch baking dish

SERVE WITH: Spinach salad with mango and feta cheese tossed with Vinaigrette

Makes 8 servings

Sopa de Maiz

2 cups chicken broth
2 boneless, skinless cooked chicken breasts, chopped
1 16-ounce bag frozen corn
$\frac{1}{2}$ teaspoon cumin
$\frac{1}{2}$ teaspoon crushed garlic
2 chicken bouillon cubes
1 4-ounce can diced green chilies
1 cup milk*
salt and pepper to taste
Fritos*
1 tomato, chopped*
1 avocado, chopped*
Salsa*
Sour cream (or plain low-fat yogurt)*

Combine first 7 ingredients in a 6-cup container and freeze.

When preparing to serve, thaw the soup and bring just to boiling. Add milk and simmer until soup is heated through. Season with salt and pepper.

In individual bowls, layer a small handful of crushed Fritos in the bottom of the bowl, then layer chopped tomatoes and diced avocado. Then pour soup over all. Add dollop each of salsa and sour cream.

SUMMARY OF PROCESSES:

Chop 2 boneless, skinless cooked chicken breasts.

FREEZE IN: 6-cup container
SERVE WITH: Mango and Avocado; Barbie's White Chocolate Chip Macadamia Nut Cookies

Makes 5 to 6 servings

Chicken Nuggets

2 pounds boneless, skinless chicken breasts, cooked and chopped

3 tablespoons butter, melted

2 teaspoons Worcestershire sauce

$\frac{1}{2}$ cup dried bread crumbs, Italian style

$\frac{1}{3}$ cup grated Parmesan cheese

Barbecue sauce (for dipping)*

Cut chicken into 1-inch pieces (kitchen shears work best). Combine chicken, melted butter, and Worcestershire in a 1-quart freezer bag to make a marinade. Combine the bread crumbs and Parmesan cheese in a second freezer bag. Tape the two bags together. Label and freeze.

To prepare for serving, thaw and remove the chicken pieces from marinade. Shake them in the bread crumb bag to coat, a few at a time. Preheat oven to 450°F. Arrange chicken on a greased cookie sheet. Bake for 7 to 9 minutes or until no longer pink in the center.

SUMMARY OF PROCESSES:

Cut 2 pounds boneless, skinless chicken into 1-inch pieces.

FREEZE IN: 1-gallon bag; 1-quart bag

SERVE WITH: Barbecue sauce for dipping; Steamed Edamame

Makes 4 to 6 servings

Herbed Chicken

  2 pounds boneless, skinless chicken breast halves
  1 $10\frac{3}{4}$-ounce can cream of mushroom soup
  1 teaspoon grated lemon zest
$1\frac{1}{2}$ tablespoons lemon juice
 $\frac{1}{2}$ teaspoon salt
  1 teaspoon dried basil leaves
  1 teaspoon dried oregano leaves
  3 cups white rice, cooked (store uncooked)*

Place chicken in a 1-gallon freezer bag. In a small bowl, combine the remaining ingredients, except rice. Pour over the chicken and freeze.

To prepare for serving, thaw chicken mixture. Preheat oven to 350°F. Place mixture in a 13×9×2-inch baking dish, treated with nonstick spray. Bake, covered, for $1\frac{1}{4}$ hours. Serve over rice.

SUMMARY OF PROCESSES:

Grate 1 tablespoon lemon zest.

FREEZE IN: 1-gallon bag
SERVE WITH: Oven-Roasted Broccoli; Reese's Chewy Chocolate Cookies

Makes 6 servings

Country Captain

1 14½-ounce can stewed tomatoes (undrained)
¼ cup fresh parsley, chopped
¼ cup currants or raisins
1 tablespoon curry powder
1 chicken bouillon cube
½ teaspoon ground mace or nutmeg
¼ teaspoon sugar
1 teaspoon salt
2 pounds boneless, skinless chicken breast halves
1 tablespoon cornstarch
1 tablespoon cold water
Cooked couscous (to serve 6; store uncooked)*
Slivered almonds (opt.)

In a medium bowl, stir together tomatoes, parsley, currants or raisins, curry pow-der, bouillon cube, mace or nutmeg, sugar, and salt. Pour over chicken in freezer bag. Label and freeze.

To prepare for serving, place thawed chicken and sauce in large skillet. Bring mixture to a boil; reduce heat. Cover and simmer for 20 minutes or until chicken is no longer pink. Remove chicken from skillet; keep warm. Skim fat from mixture in skillet. In a small bowl stir together cornstarch and cold water; add to skillet. Cook and stir till thickened and bubbly. Cook and stir 2 minutes more. Serve over hot rice or couscous. Sprinkle with almonds, if desired.

SUMMARY OF PROCESSES:
Chop ¼ cup fresh parsley.

FREEZE IN: 1-gallon bag
SERVE WITH: Seasonal fresh fruit salad

Makes 6 servings

Denise's Black Beans

1 pound smoked sausage cut into pieces
3 15-ounce cans black beans, drained
1½ cups chopped onion
1½ cups chopped green bell pepper
1½ cups chopped celery
2 teaspoons crushed garlic
2 teaspoons dried thyme leaves
1½ teaspoons dried oregano leaves
1½ teaspoons pepper
¼ teaspoon cayenne pepper
1 chicken bouillon cube
5 bay leaves
1 8-ounce can tomato sauce
1 cup water
4 cups white rice, cooked (store uncooked)*

Combine all ingredients, except rice, in a Crock-Pot. Cook on low for 6 hours. Remove bay leaves. Cool to room temperature and freeze.

When preparing to serve, heat to boiling and simmer 15 minutes. Serve over hot, cooked rice.

SUMMARY OF PROCESSES:

Chop 1½ cups onion, 1½ cups green pepper, and 1½ cups celery; cut smoked sausages into pieces.

SERVE WITH: Crudités
FREEZE IN: 1 6-cup container

Makes 8 servings

Winter Pot Roast

1 $2\frac{1}{2}$ pound beef roast
2 tablespoons steak sauce
2 medium onions thinly sliced
1 15-ounce can tomato sauce
1 cup catsup
1 teaspoon salt
2 teaspoons sugar
$\frac{1}{4}$ teaspoon pepper
$1\frac{1}{2}$ tablespoons pure horseradish
8 new potatoes*

Combine all ingredients except roast and potatoes. Pour over roast in a 1-gallon freezer bag. Seal and freeze.

Thaw and place the contents into Crock-Pot. Cover and cook on low for 6 to 8 hours. Check every few hours to make sure there is enough fluid. Cut meat into cubes and put back into sauce. Serve on boiled potatoes topped with chopped parsley.

FREEZE IN: 1-gallon bag
SERVE WITH: Broiled Tomatoes

Makes 6 servings

Poppy Beef

 2 pounds ground beef
 $\frac{1}{2}$ cup chopped green pepper
 $\frac{1}{2}$ teaspoon salt
 $\frac{1}{2}$ cup chopped onion
 1 15-ounce can tomato sauce
 8 ounces cottage cheese
 1 tablespoon poppy seeds
 1 cup plain low-fat yogurt
 8 ounces light cream cheese
 $\frac{1}{4}$ teaspoon pepper
 8 ounces linguine*
 $\frac{1}{4}$ cup grated Parmesan cheese*

Saute the beef with green pepper, salt, and onion in a large skillet on medium heat until the beef is no longer pink, about 15 minutes. Add tomato sauce and set aside. Combine the remaining ingredients in a medium bowl, except linguini and Parmesan cheese. Freeze each of the two mixtures in gallon bags taped together.

When preparing to serve, thaw the bags. Preheat oven to 350°F. Cook 8 ounces linguini according to package directions and drain. While pasta is hot, mix it into the cheese mixture in a medium bowl. Spread the linguini and cheese on the bottom of a greased casserole dish. Top with the meat mixture and sprinkle with Parmesan cheese. Bake for 30 minutes or until hot and bubbly.

SUMMARY OF PROCESSES:

Chop $\frac{1}{2}$ cup green pepper; chop $\frac{1}{2}$ cup onion.

FREEZE IN: 2 1-gallon bags
SERVE WITH: Apple-Spinach Salad

Makes 8 servings

Playoff Burgers

2 pounds lean ground beef
1 onion, chopped
1 tablespoon steak sauce
1 cup grated Monterey Jack cheese
Salt and pepper to taste
6 whole wheat buns*

Salt and pepper ground beef to taste and mix with chopped onion and A-1 sauce. Make 12 thin patties. Sprinkle cheese over 6 of these, then top with remaining 6 patties and press edges together. Wrap each patty in waxed paper and seal them in a 1-gallon freezer bag. Label the bag and freeze. Freeze the package of whole wheat buns.

To prepare for serving, thaw patties and place on the rack of a broiler pan. Broil 3 to 4 inches from the heat for a total of 12 to 14 minutes or until done, turning once. Serve on thawed whole wheat buns, split and toasted.

SUMMARY OF PROCESSES:

Chop 1 onion.

FREEZE IN: 1-gallon bag
SERVE WITH: Crudités and chips
NOTE: Great on the grill or for camping trips.

Makes 6 servings

London Broil

    1 London broil (about 2 pounds)
    1 teaspoon ground ginger
    1 tablespoon grated lemon zest
    1 tablespoon vegetable oil
    $\frac{1}{2}$ teaspoon crushed garlic
    1 teaspoon black pepper
    1 teaspoon light brown sugar

In a shallow bowl large enough to hold the steak, stir all ingredients (except London broil) together, making a marinade. Turn the steak in the marinade, rubbing the ingredients into the meat. Put steak and marinade in a freezer bag, label and freeze.

To prepare for serving, thaw steak and discard marinade. Grill over hot coals 4 to 5 minutes per side. Do not overcook or steak becomes tough (serving rare is best). Carve slices on the bias.

SUMMARY OF PROCESSES:

Grate 1 tablespoon lemon zest.

FREEZE IN: 1-gallon bag
SERVE WITH: Twice-Baked Sweet Potatoes

Makes 5 servings

French Stuffed Potatoes

1 pound lean ground beef
$\frac{1}{4}$ cup chopped green onion
1 4-ounce can mushroom stems and pieces
$\frac{1}{2}$ teaspoon salt
$\frac{1}{2}$ teaspoon onion salt
$\frac{1}{2}$ cup grated Swiss cheese
$\frac{1}{2}$ cup grated Cheddar cheese
1 large baking potato*

Brown together in a skillet the ground beef, green onion, and mushrooms. Add the salt and onion salt.

Freeze the meat mixture in a freezer bag. Store the grated cheeses in a small bag and tape the smaller bag to the larger one. Store the potatoes until serving the dish.

When preparing to serve, thaw the meat mixture and cheeses. Preheat oven to 400°F. Bake the potato for 1 hour at 400°F or until done. When the potato is nearly done, heat the meat mixture in a small saucepan or skillet.

Slice open the potatoes, break up potatoes with a fork, and spoon the meat mixture and cheese atop each potato. Return to the oven until cheese is melted.

SUMMARY OF PROCESSES:

Chop $\frac{1}{4}$ cup green onions.

FREEZE IN: 1-gallon bag; 1-quart bag
SERVE WITH: Caesar salad

Makes 4 servings

Spaghetti Soup

  1 pound Italian sausage browned and drained
  1 26-ounce jar marinara sauce
  1 14.5-ounce can diced tomatoes, drained
  1 large green bell pepper, diced
  1 large onion, chopped
  1 cup water
$1\frac{1}{2}$ teaspoons fennel seeds
  1 tablespoon basil
 12 ounces dry extra-thick noodles stored in small Ziploc bag
$1\frac{1}{2}$ cups shredded mozzarella stored in small Ziploc bag

Combine all ingredients except dry noodles and cheese. Place in bag and label. Tape bag of noodles and bag of cheese to sauce bag and freeze.

Thaw. Pour both sauce and noodles into slow cooker and cover. Cook 5 to 6 hours on low. Ladle into soup bowl and top with mozzarella cheese.

SUMMARY OF PROCESSES:
Chop 1 large onion and 1 large green bell pepper.

FREEZE IN: 1-gallon bag; 2-1-quart bags
SERVE WITH: Green salad tossed with Creamy Dressing

Makes 6 servings

Farmer's Casserole

6 cups frozen shredded hash brown potatoes

1 cup grated Monterey Jack cheese with jalapeño peppers

1 cup diced fully cooked ham

$\frac{1}{4}$ cup sliced green onion

4 beaten large eggs

1 12-ounce can evaporated milk or evaporated skim milk

$\frac{1}{8}$ teaspoon pepper

$\frac{1}{4}$ teaspoon salt

Grease a 13×9×2-inch baking dish. Arrange potatoes evenly in the bottom of the dish. Sprinkle with cheese, ham, and green onion.

In a medium mixing bowl combine eggs, evaporated milk, pepper, and salt. Pour egg mixture over potato mixture in dish. Freeze.

To prepare to serve, thaw and preheat oven to 350°F. Bake, uncovered, for 40 to 45 minutes or until center appears set. Let stand 5 minutes before serving.

SUMMARY OF PROCESSES:

Dice 1 cup ham; slice $\frac{1}{4}$ cup green onions.

FREEZE IN: 13×9×2-inch baking dish
SERVE WITH: Spiced applesauce; coffee cake

Makes 8 servings

5

One-Month Entrée Plan D

Grocery Shopping and Staples Lists

An asterisk (*) after an item indicates that it can be stored until you cook the dish with which it will be served. For example, the spaghetti will not be cooked until the day you serve spaghetti. Mark those items with an "X" as a reminder that you'll need them for an entrée.

When entrées require perishable food to be refrigerated until served, you may want to use those dishes right away or buy the food the week you plan to prepare the dish. For example, fresh mushrooms would spoil within a couple of weeks.

For this one-month entrée plan, you will need these food items as well as the ones in the staples list that follows.

GROCERY SHOPPING LIST

CANNED GOODS

1 15-ounce can apricots

3 cups apple juice

1 16-ounce can whole berry cranberry sauce

3 14½-ounce cans beef broth

1 12-ounce bottle stout beer

1 8-ounce bottle chile sauce

1 10¾-ounce can condensed cream of mushroom soup

3 4-ounce cans diced, green chilies

3 15-ounce cans red kidney beans

1 4-ounce can mushroom stems and pieces

2 15-ounce cans diced tomatoes

4 28-ounce cans Italian-style or plain crushed tomatoes in puree

3 6-ounce cans tomato paste

2 8-ounce cans tomato sauce

3 6-ounce cans sliced water chestnuts

½ cup Dijon mustard

GRAINS, PASTA, AND RICE

1 loaf unsliced French bread (not sourdough)*

6 hamburger buns*

4 sandwich rolls*

1 15-ounce container Italian-flavored bread crumbs*

1 16-ounce package spaghetti*

1 8-ounce package spinach noodles or wide egg noodles

1 1.25-ounce envelope dried onion soup

1 8-ounce package tortellini*

1 6¼-ounce package long-grain and wild rice (Uncle Ben's Fast-Cooking
    Long-Grain and Wild Rice, if available)

1 16-ounce package regular rice

1 16-ounce package linguine

DRY INGREDIENTS AND SEASONINGS

⅓ cup raisins

1 1.25-ounce envelope onion soup mix

1 package taco seasoning mix

1½ cups (about) seasoned croutons

FROZEN FOODS

4 frozen fish fillets (about $1\frac{1}{4}$ pounds) (orange roughy or sole)

1 $1\frac{1}{2}$-pound salmon fillet

2 9-inch, deep-dish frozen pie shells (1*)

1 13-ounce package plain ravioli without sauce* (located in the frozen or refrigerated section)

1 10-ounce package frozen, chopped spinach

DAIRY PRODUCTS

1 cup butter

2 packages refrigerated crescent rolls*

7 large eggs

1 cup half-and-half

2 quarts milk (whole, 2%, or skim)

18 ounces grated, mild Cheddar cheese

3 ounces cream cheese

5 ounces grated Monterey Jack cheese

8 ounces mozzarella cheese (4 in slices, the remainder grated)

4 ounces grated Parmesan cheese

4 ounces grated Swiss cheese

2 8-ounce containers sour cream or plain low-fat yogurt

MEAT AND POULTRY

1 4-to-6-pound beef brisket

$5\frac{1}{2}$ pounds lean ground beef (allow 1 pound for hamburgers; buy more if needed for your family)

$\frac{1}{2}$ pound ground turkey

9 pounds whole chickens or 7 pounds breasts

$5\frac{3}{4}$ pounds boneless, skinless chicken breasts

5 pounds chicken pieces (breasts, drumsticks, or thighs)

5 pounds boneless, cooked ham (3 pounds sliced ham)

1 pound bulk Italian sausage meat

1 pound very thin, boneless veal cutlets* (or substitute 1 pound boneless, skinless chicken breasts)

1 3-ounce-package sliced pepperoni (use half)

4 slices of bacon

2 pounds pork tenderloin

2 pounds London broil

3 pounds cured corned beef brisket

2 pounds beef stew meat cut into bite-size pieces

PRODUCE

10 medium carrots

8 medium baking potatoes*

8 to 10 new potatoes*

3 tomatoes*

1 bunch celery

1 4.5-ounce jar crushed garlic

1 small lemon*

1 small head of lettuce

1 small bunch green onions

1 medium green bell pepper

1 medium red bell pepper

$6\frac{1}{2}$ pounds (about 10) yellow onions

1 bunch fresh parsley

STAPLES LIST

Make sure you have the following staples on hand; add those you don't have to your shopping list.

basil leaves, dried

bay leaves

biscuit baking mix (1 cup)

catsup

celery seeds

chili powder

cilantro (optional)

cloves (whole)

cumin, ground

curry powder

Dijon mustard

dried dill weed

flour, all-purpose

garlic powder

garlic salt

ginger, ground

lemon juice (about $\frac{2}{3}$ cup)

    lemon pepper
    light brown sugar
    light mayonnaise (about 2 cups)
    minced onion
    dried mustard (1 teaspoon)
    prepared mustard
    nonstick spray
    onion salt
    dried oregano leaves
    paprika
    pepper
    peppercorns (6)
    kosher salt
    salt
    soda crackers (1 cup crumbs)
    soy sauce
    sugar
    dried thyme leaves
    vegetable oil
    red wine vinegar
    white vinegar
    waxed paper
    Worcestershire sauce

Freezer Containers

The following list of freezer containers or flat baking dishes will be needed for the entrées. These are not the only containers you can use, but this list gives you an idea of the size and number of containers you'll need. Labeling containers before you cook works best.

    Heavy Aluminum Foil: French-Bread Pizza

13 1-quart freezer bags: French-Bread Pizza (3); Chicken Packets (2); Veal Scallopini in Spaghetti Sauce (2); Heavenly Chicken (1); Taco Pie (1); Meal-in-One Potatoes (1); Baked Herb Fish Fillets (1); Brine for Salmon (1); Marinade for London Broil (1); Veggies and Spices for Beer Corned Beef (1)

One-Month Entrée Plan D

SUN.	MON.	TUES.	WED.	THURS.	FRI.	SAT.
	1 — Eat Out Cooking Day!	2 — Mrs. Ringle's Brisket	3 — Easy Stroganoff	4 — Spaghetti Sauce	5 — Veal Scallopini	6 — French-Bread Pizza
7 — Ham-and-Swiss Pastry Bake	8 — Ham Dinner Slices	9 — Stove-Top Barbecued Chicken	10 — Wild Rice Chicken	11 — Teriyaki Burgers	12 — Chicken Packets	13 — Heavenly Chicken
14 — Chicken Chili	15 — Asian Chicken	16 — Mimi's Chicken Soup	17 — Meal-in-One Potatoes	18 — Fruity Curried Chicken	19 — Bacon-Wrapped Meat Loaf	20 — Joes to Go
21 — Ravioli Soup	22 — Taco Pie	23 — Baked Herb Fish Fillets	24 — Aztec Quiche	25 — Mustard Barbecued Chicken	26 — Brined Salmon Fillet	27 — Slow Cooker Fall Pork Roast
28 — London Broil in Marinade	29 — Slow Cooker Beer Corned Beef	30 — Slow Cooker Beef Goulash				

16 1-gallon freezer bags: Mrs. Ringle's Brisket (1); Easy Stroganoff (1); Veal Scallopini (1); Ham-and-Swiss Pastry Bake (1); Wild Rice Chicken (1); Bacon-Wrapped Meatloaf (1); Ham Dinner Slices (1); Teriyaki Burgers (1); Asian Chicken (1); Baked Herb Fish Fillets (1); Mustard Barbecued Chicken (1); Chicken Chili (1); Beer Corned Beef (1); Slow Cooker Beef Goulash (1); Slow Cooker Fall Pork Roast (1), London Broil (1)

2 3-cup containers: Veal Scallopini in Spaghetti Sauce; French-Bread Pizza

3 4-cup containers: Fruity Curried Chicken; Spaghetti Sauce; Stove-Top Barbecued Chicken

2 8-cup containers: Joes to Go; Mimi's Chicken Soup

1 10-cup container: Ravioli Soup

2 13×9×2-inch baking dishes: Heavenly Chicken; Last-Minute Lasagna

2 9-inch quiche or pie pan: Aztec Quiche; Ham and Swiss Pastry Bake

1 10-inch quiche or pie pan: Taco Pie

The Day Before Cooking Day

1. Cut $1\frac{1}{2}$ pounds of boneless chicken breasts into 1-inch cubes with kitchen scissors and refrigerate. Refrigerate remaining boneless chicken breasts and 2 pounds of chicken pieces.
2. Refrigerate lemon and store baking and new potatoes (unrefrigerated) until you're ready to serve them.
3. Place 9 pounds whole chickens (or 7 pounds breasts) in about 6 quarts water in a large pot (you may need two). Bring to a boil; reduce heat. Cover and simmer until thickest pieces are done, about 45 minutes to 1 hour. Save and refrigerate $3\frac{1}{4}$ quarts chicken broth. Cool chicken until ready to handle. Remove meat from bones and skin. Cut chicken into bite-size pieces using kitchen scissors, which are easier to use than a knife. Refrigerate chicken pieces in two plastic bags.
4. Put Ham Dinner Slices, hamburger buns, and sandwich rolls in freezer bags, mark bags with names of recipes; store them in freezer until you're ready to serve them.
5. For Veal Scaloppine in Spaghetti Sauce, put veal cutlets in 1-gallon freezer bag, Italian-flavored bread crumbs and mozzarella cheese in separate 1-quart freezer bags; freeze them together.

6. For French-Bread Pizza, put pepperoni in 1-quart freezer bag, $\frac{1}{4}$ cup grated Parmesan cheese and 1 cup grated mozzarella cheese in separate 1-quart freezer bags, wrap French bread in heavy foil and put them together in freezer.

7. Set out appliances, bowls, canned goods, dry ingredients, freezer containers, and recipes.

8. Start Mrs. Ringle's Brisket in a Crock-Pot (just before bed).

On Cooking Day, Before Assembling Dishes

1. Make sure you've cleared the table and counters of unnecessary kitchenware to allow plenty of working room. It also helps to have fresh, damp washcloths and towels for wiping your hands and the cooking area. The day will go a lot more smoothly if you keep cleaning and organizing as you work.

2. Before you prepare a recipe, gather all the spices and ingredients in the assembly area to save time and steps. When you finish the recipe, remove unneeded items and wipe off the work space.

3. Cool, slice, and divide brisket and gravy in half for Mrs. Ringle's Brisket and Easy Stroganoff. Put brisket in two 1-gallon bags and freeze them. Wash out Crock-Pot.

4. Skim and discard fat from chicken broth.

5. Perform all chopping, crushing, grating, and slicing tasks.

   Ham: Cut 3 cups into cubes.

   Onions: Leave one onion whole for Mimi's Chicken Soup; finely chop remaining onions. Open windows, and keep tissues handy. Store onions in cold water in a container with a tight lid.

   Green onions: Chop $\frac{1}{2}$ cup (cut in 2 tablespoons of the green part).

   Green bell peppers: Chop.

   Red bell pepper: Chop.

   Carrots: Shred 3, slice 7.

   Celery: Slice $\frac{1}{2}$ cup with leaves; finely chop $1\frac{3}{4}$ cups.

   Parsley: Chop $\frac{2}{3}$ cup.

   Mozzarella cheese: Cut 4 slices; grate the rest.

   Cracker crumbs: Crush 1 cup.

6. Start Spaghetti Sauce.

7. Spray pans or baking dishes you will need with nonstick spray.

8. As you assemble the ham, chicken, beef, and miscellaneous entrees, allow them to cool if necessary, put them in storage containers, and freeze them.

Assembly Order

ASSEMBLE HAM DISHES

1. Assemble Ham and Swiss Pastry Bake.
2. Finish Ham Dinner Slices.
3. Freeze ham dishes.

ASSEMBLE POULTRY DISHES

1. Prepare Stove-Top Barbecued Chicken in a skillet, and simmer.
2. In separate saucepans, cook rice for Wild Rice Chicken and the $\frac{3}{4}$ cup regular rice for Fruity Curried Chicken according to package directions.
3. Make filling for Chicken Packets in a medium bowl (mixing with hands works best), and put in a freezer bag.
4. Finish assembling Wild Rice Chicken and Fruity Curried Chicken.
5. Prepare Heavenly Chicken.
6. Prepare Chicken Chili.
7. Assemble Asian Chicken.
8. Assemble Mustard Barbecued Chicken.
9. Prepare Mimi's Chicken Soup with remaining chicken broth and start simmering.
10. Assemble filling for Meal-in-One Potatoes.
11. Freeze poultry dishes.

ASSEMBLE BEEF DISHES

1. Assemble Teriyaki Burgers.
2. Complete Bacon-Wrapped Meat Loaf.
3. In a large skillet, cook and stir $3\frac{1}{2}$ pounds lean ground beef until brown, about 30 minutes.
4. In a small skillet, sauté $1\frac{1}{2}$ cup chopped onions until tender; use for Taco Pie and Joes to Go.
5. Assemble Ravioli Soup, start it simmering.
6. Put Spaghetti Sauce in freezer containers according to directions. Put containers of sauce for Veal Scallopini in Spaghetti Sauce and French-Bread Pizza in freezer with already packaged items for those dishes.
7. Assemble Taco Pie.

8. Prepare Joes to Go and Bacon-Wrapped Meat Loaf.
9. Allow Mimi's Chicken Soup and Ravioli Soup to cool and store in freezer containers.
10. Freeze beef dishes.

ASSEMBLE MISCELLANEOUS DISHES

1. Prepare Baked Herb Fish Fillets coating mix.
2. Complete Aztec Quiche.
3. Prepare brine for salmon.
4. Assemble Fall Pork Roast.
5. Prepare London Broil marinade.
6. Assemble Slow Cooker Corned Beef.
7. Assemble Slow Cooker Beef Goulash.
8. Cool Spaghetti Sauce.
9. Freeze miscellaneous dishes.

You made it! Hooray!!

Recipes for the One-Month Entrée Plan D

Each recipe offers complete instructions on how to prepare the dish. Food items with an asterisk (*) won't be prepared until you serve the entrée. For recipes calling for oven baking, preheat oven for about 10 minutes.

"Summary of processes" gives a quick overview of foods that need to be chopped, diced, grated, or sliced. "Freeze in" tells what bags and containers will be needed to freeze each entrée. "Serve with" offers suggestions of foods to accompany the meal. Some of the recipes for those foods are included in chapter 8; page numbers are indicated for easy reference. "Note" includes special instructions on how the entrée can be used in other ways.

Mrs. Ringle's Brisket

　　1　4- to-6-pound brisket
　　2　tablespoons prepared mustard
　　1　envelope dried onion soup
　　4　to 5 new potatoes*
　　Flour (optional)

Place brisket fat side up in a Crock-Pot. Do not add any water or liquid. Cover brisket with mustard and dry onion soup mix. Cook on low overnight.

Skim mustard and onion seasoning from brisket and mix it with juice in the Crock-Pot. Remove brisket from Crock-Pot, allow to cool. Peel off fat and discard it; slice or shred meat. Save juices and seasonings (thicken with flour to make gravy, if desired). Divide meat and gravy in half, and store in separate 1-gallon bags in freezer. Reserve 1 bag for Mrs. Ringle's Brisket and one for Easy Stroganoff.

To prepare for serving, thaw brisket and gravy and heat. At the same time, prepare new potatoes. Heat 1 cup salted water to a boil; add potatoes. Cover and heat until boiling; reduce heat. Simmer tightly covered until tender, 20 to 25 minutes; drain. Serve potatoes with brisket and gravy.

FREEZE IN: 2 1-gallon bags
SERVE WITH: Corn on the cob; Cauliflower Mock Potato Salad

Makes 4 to 5 servings

Easy Stroganoff

　　Half of gravy and sliced brisket from Mrs. Ringle's Brisket
　　1　8-ounce container sour cream*
　　linguine (16-ounce package)

Thaw brisket slices; heat them in the gravy. Add sour cream.

SERVE WITH: Linguine and Watermelon Salad

Makes 4 to 6 servings

Spaghetti Sauce

    1 pound bulk Italian sausage
1½ cups finely chopped onion
    2 6-ounce cans tomato paste
    3 28-ounce cans Italian-style or plain crushed tomatoes in puree
    2 cups water
    4 teaspoons minced garlic
    4 bay leaves
    2 tablespoons sugar
    4 teaspoons dried basil leaves
    2 teaspoons dried oregano leaves
  ¼ cup chopped fresh parsley
    2 teaspoons salt
    1 16-ounce package spaghetti*

    In a large pot, cook and stir the bulk Italian sausage with onions until the meat is brown, about 15 minutes; drain fat. Add remaining ingredients, except the spaghetti. Bring sauce to a boil; reduce heat. Partly cover and simmer for 2 hours, stirring occasionally. (If desired, simmer in a Crock-Pot instead.) Makes 12 cups sauce.

    Allow sauce to cool. Freeze.

    To prepare Spaghetti, thaw 4 cups sauce, and heat in a medium saucepan. At the same time, cook spaghetti according to package directions, drain, and pour sauce over them.

SUMMARY OF PROCESSES:

    Chop 1½ cups onions, ¼ cup parsley.

FREEZE IN: 4-cup container, Spaghetti Sauce; 2 3-cup containers French-Bread Pizza and Veal Scaloppine in Spaghetti Sauce

SERVE WITH: For variety try serving sauce on cooked Spaghetti Squash instead of the noodles. Green salad tossed in Creamy Dressing will give extra color to this yummy meal

Makes 6 servings

Veal Scallopini in Spaghetti Sauce

1 pound thin veal cutlets (or substitute 1 pound boneless, skinless chicken breasts)*

2½ cups spaghetti sauce*

1 large egg*

¾ cup Italian-flavored bread crumbs*

3 tablespoons vegetable or olive oil*

1 teaspoon minced garlic

4 slices mozzarella cheese*

Grated Parmesan cheese*

This recipe is assembled on the day it's served. On cooking day put veal cutlets in 1-gallon bag; Spaghetti Sauce in a 3-cup container; Italian-flavored breadcrumbs and mozzarella cheese in separate 1-quart bags, and freeze them together.

Thaw veal cutlets, bread crumbs, cheese slices, and container of Spaghetti Sauce. Beat egg with fork until white and yolk are blended. Sprinkle Italian-flavored bread crumbs on a sheet of waxed paper. Dip veal into egg and then crumbs, turning to coat both sides evenly.

In a large skillet, heat oil with garlic over medium or medium-high heat. Add veal; sauté 4 minutes on each side, until golden brown. Top each piece of veal with a cheese slice.

Pour Spaghetti Sauce around veal. Bring sauce to boil; reduce heat. Cover and simmer 5 minutes or until cheese is melted. Sprinkle Parmesan cheese on top.

SUMMARY OF PROCESSES:

Slice 4 slices mozzarella cheese.

FREEZE IN: 3-cup container; 1-gallon bag; and 2 1-quart bags
SERVE WITH: Greek Pasta Salad French bread

Makes 4 servings

French-Bread Pizza

1 loaf unsliced French bread (not sourdough)*
3 cups spaghetti sauce*
$\frac{1}{4}$ cup grated Parmesan cheese*
1 cup grated mozzarella cheese*
3 ounces pepperoni slices*

This recipe is assembled on the day it's served. Put sauce in a 3-cup container, cheeses in 2 1-quart bags, pepperoni in 1-quart bag; wrap bread in heavy foil. Freeze them together.

To prepare for serving, thaw French bread, sauce, grated cheeses, and pepperoni. Slice loaf of French bread in half lengthwise. Layer sauce, Parmesan cheese, pepperoni, and mozzarella cheese on each half. Set oven to broil and/or 550°F. Place bread on baking sheet and put in the oven. Broil until mozzarella is melted. Cut into serving-size pieces.

FREEZE IN: 3-cup container; 3 1-quart bags; foil for bread
SERVE WITH: Great meal to have when you have to go out for dinner. The children will love munching on Steamed Edamame, and enjoy Barbie's White Chocolate Chip Macadarnia Cookies for dessert.

Makes 6 to 8 servings

Ham-and-Swiss Pastry Bake

2 cups cooked, cubed ham

1 cup grated Swiss cheese

$\frac{1}{4}$ cup finely chopped celery

$\frac{1}{4}$ cup finely chopped green bell pepper

2 tablespoons minced onion

1 teaspoon dried mustard

1 tablespoon lemon juice

$\frac{1}{3}$ cup light mayonnaise or salad dressing*

1 9-inch deep-dish frozen pie shell*

Combine ham, cheese, celery, bell pepper, onion, mustard, and lemon juice in a 1-gallon plastic bag and store in freezer.

To prepare for serving, thaw ham mixture, add mayonnaise, and put into a 9-inch pie shell. Bake uncovered in a preheated 375°F oven for 25 to 35 minutes until golden brown. Serve hot.

SUMMARY OF PROCESSES:

Cut 2 cups ham into cubes; grate 1 cup Swiss cheese; chop $\frac{1}{4}$ cup celery and $\frac{1}{4}$ cup bell pepper.

FREEZE IN: 1-gallon bag

SERVE WITH: French-cut green beans—cook and toss them with toasted sliced almonds.

Makes 6 servings

Ham Dinner Slices

2 $\frac{3}{4}$-inch-thick cooked ham slices
Prepared mustard*
Light brown sugar*
1 cup milk (whole, 2%, or skim)*

Freeze ham slices in 1-gallon bag.

To serve, thaw ham slices. Wash and prick potatoes and bake in a preheated 400°F oven for about 1 hour or until done. Place ham slices in a single layer in the bottom of an 8×8×2-inch baking dish treated with nonstick spray. Spread mustard on top of each slice; sprinkle brown sugar over mustard. Pour enough milk over ham slices to come halfway up their sides. Bake uncovered 45 minutes.

FREEZE IN: 1-gallon bag
SERVE WITH: Roasted potatoes with Thai fish sauce; steamed green beans; warmed multigrain rolls

Makes 4 servings

Stove-Top Barbecued Chicken

  1 tablespoon vegetable oil
  1 cup finely chopped onion
  $\frac{1}{3}$ cup catsup
  $\frac{1}{3}$ cup water
  4 teaspoons white vinegar
  4 teaspoons light brown sugar
  $1\frac{1}{2}$ teaspoons Worcestershire sauce
  $\frac{1}{2}$ teaspoon chili powder
  $\frac{1}{4}$ teaspoon celery seeds
  2 pounds skinless chicken pieces
  1 8-ounce package spinach noodles or wide egg noodles*

Heat oil in a large, nonstick skillet; sauté onion until tender, about 10 minutes. Stir in catsup, water, vinegar, brown sugar, Worcestershire sauce, chili powder, and celery seeds. Bring sauce to a boil. Add the chicken to the skillet, placing the side down that has the skin removed; spoon sauce over the pieces. Bring to a boil; reduce heat. Cover and simmer 30 minutes. Turn chicken pieces and simmer covered for about 20 minutes more or until chicken is cooked through. Cool and freeze chicken and sauce.

To prepare for serving, thaw chicken and sauce; put in a large skillet and cook over medium heat, stirring constantly until bubbly. Cook package of spinach noodles or egg noodles according to package directions; serve chicken over noodles.

SUMMARY OF PROCESSES:

  Chop 1 cup onion.

FREEZE IN: 4-cup container
SERVE WITH: Mango and Avocado (sliced, arranged on a plate, and topped with lemon juice. Add salt and pepper if desired).

Makes 4 servings

Wild Rice Chicken

1 6¼-ounce package quick-cooking long-grain and wild rice
1 cup cooked, chopped chicken
1 8-ounce can sliced water chestnuts, drained
1 cup finely chopped celery
1¼ cups finely chopped onion
1 cup light mayonnaise*
1 10¾-ounce can condensed cream of mushroom soup*

Cook rice according to package directions. Combine rice with chopped chicken, water chestnuts, celery, and onion; put mixture in a 1-gallon freezer bag.

To prepare for serving, thaw rice and chicken mixture, remove from bag, and place in a 2½-quart baking dish. Stir mayonnaise and condensed cream of mushroom soup together and spread over top of chicken. Bake covered in a preheated 325°F oven for 1 hour.

SUMMARY OF PROCESSES:
Chop 1 cup cooked chicken, 1 cup celery, and 1¼ cups onion.

FREEZE IN: 1-gallon bag
SERVE WITH: Broiled Tomatoes; Italian Parsley Salad

Makes 6 servings

Fruity Curried Chicken

$\frac{3}{4}$ cup regular, uncooked rice
1 cup finely chopped onion
$2\frac{1}{2}$ cups chicken broth
$8\frac{3}{4}$ ounces apricots, drained
$2\frac{1}{4}$ cups cooked, diced chicken
$\frac{3}{4}$ teaspoon salt
1 teaspoon curry powder
2 teaspoons lemon juice
$\frac{1}{3}$ cup raisins

In a medium saucepan, bring rice, onion, and chicken broth to a boil, stirring once or twice. Reduce heat to low; cover and simmer 15 minutes. Do not lift lid or stir rice. Drain and cut apricots into pieces. Add the remaining ingredients. Allow to cool and store in freezer.

To prepare for serving, thaw entrée, put in baking dish, and cover with foil. Bake in a preheated 350°F oven for 1 hour. (Add a small amount of water if it becomes too dry after baking.)

SUMMARY OF PROCESSES:

Chop 1 cup onion and $2\frac{1}{2}$ cups cooked chicken.

FREEZE IN: 4-cup container
SERVE WITH: Steamed broccoli, and just before serving toss with toasted sesame seeds; Watermelon Salad would complete this meal nicely.

Makes 4 servings

Chicken Packets

 2 cups cooked, chopped chicken
 3 ounces cream cheese, softened
 1 tablespoon of the green part of the green onion, chopped fine
 2 tablespoons milk (whole, 2%, or skim)
 Salt to taste
 $\frac{1}{2}$ cup crushed, seasoned crouton crumbs*
 2 packages refrigerated crescent rolls*
 $\frac{1}{4}$ cup melted butter*

Mix chicken, cream cheese, chives, milk, and salt in a medium bowl (mixing with hands works best) to make filling and store in a 1-quart freezer bag. Put crouton crumbs in another 1-quart bag, attach it to bag of chicken filling, and freeze them both. Refrigerate crescent rolls.

To prepare for serving, thaw chicken mixture. Unroll crescent rolls. Each tube will contain 4 rectangles of dough with a diagonal perforation. Press dough along each perforation so that the rectangle halves will not separate. Place about $\frac{1}{4}$ cup of chicken mixture into the center of each rectangle. Fold dough over the filling and pinch the edges to seal tightly. Dip each packet in melted butter and coat with crouton crumbs. Place packets on a baking sheet. Bake in a preheated 350°F oven for 20 minutes or until golden brown. Packets are good either hot or cold. (Serve early in the month before date expires on crescent rolls.) Makes 8 packets.

SUMMARY OF PROCESSES:
 Chop 2 cups cooked chicken and 1 tablespoon green part of green onions.

 FREEZE IN: 2 1-quart bags
 SERVE WITH: Crudités; Reese's Chewy Chocolate Cookies
 NOTE: These packets are a favorite with children.

Makes 4 to 6 servings

Heavenly Chicken

1 10-ounce-package frozen, chopped spinach—squeezed to drain water
8 boneless chicken breast halves, skinned (about 3¼ pounds)
1 cup cooked, cubed ham
1 cup soda cracker crumbs
1 cup grated Parmesan cheese

WHITE SAUCE
½ cup sliced green onions
2 tablespoons butter
2 tablespoons all-purpose flour
1 cup milk (whole, 2%, or skim)

In a medium saucepan, make White Sauce; sauté onions in butter over low heat until tender, about 5 minutes. Stir in flour and add milk all at once. Cook over low heat, stirring constantly until bubbly. Boil and stir 1 minute more until smooth and thickened.

Combine cracker crumbs and cheese. Dip chicken breasts in soda cracker crumbs to coat lightly. Arrange breast halves in a 13×9×2-inch baking dish. Seal leftover crumb mixture in a 1-quart bag.

Stir spinach and ham into White Sauce, spoon sauce over chicken breasts. Allow to cool and cover baking dish with foil, attaching bag of crumb mixture to side of dish.

To prepare for serving, thaw dish and bake covered in a preheated 350°F oven for 60 to 75 minutes. Uncover and sprinkle top with reserved soda cracker crumbs. Bake 10 minutes more.

SUMMARY OF PROCESSES:
Slice ½ cup green onions; crush 1 cup soda cracker; cut 1 cup ham into cubes.

FREEZE IN: 13×9×2-inch baking dish; 1-quart bag
SERVE WITH: Pineapple chunks and mandarin oranges tossed with toasted shredded coconut

Makes 8 servings

Chicken Chili

$\frac{1}{2}$ pound boneless skinless chicken breasts
1 medium onion, chopped
2 teaspoons minced garlic
2 15-ounce cans kidney beans, drained
1 15-ounce can diced tomatoes, not drained
1 4-ounce can diced green chilies
$\frac{1}{2}$ cup water
1 tablespoon dried cilantro (optional)
2 teaspoons chili powder
$1\frac{1}{2}$ teaspoons cumin

Cut the chicken into bite-size pieces, then brown in saucepan coated with non-stick cooking spray. Add the remaining ingredients, cover and simmer for 30 minutes or until chicken is tender.

SUMMARY OF PROCESSES:
Cut chicken into bite-size pieces; chop 1 medium onion.

FREEZE IN: 1-gallon bag
SERVE WITH: Corn chips; Hearts of Palm Salad

Makes 4 to 5 servings

Asian Chicken

  1 pound boneless, skinless chicken breasts
  1 cup regular, uncooked rice*

MARINADE

  $\frac{1}{2}$ cup soy sauce
  $\frac{1}{2}$ cup sugar
  $1\frac{1}{4}$ tablespoons red wine vinegar
  2 teaspoons vegetable oil
  $\frac{1}{2}$ teaspoon minced garlic
  $\frac{3}{4}$ teaspoon ground ginger

Mix soy sauce, sugar, vinegar, oil, garlic, and ginger to make the marinade (reserve 2 tablespoons in a small bowl for Teriyaki Burgers). Freeze chicken in marinade in a 1-gallon bag.

When preparing to serve, thaw chicken. Pour chicken and marinade into a baking dish. Bake in a preheated 350°F oven for 35 minutes. Prepare rice according to package directions. Serve chicken over rice.

  FREEZE IN: 1-gallon bag
  SERVE WITH: Apple-Spinach Salad; French bread

Makes 4 servings

Mimi's Chicken Soup

1 small onion
2 or 3 whole cloves
1 cup cooked, diced chicken
2 quarts chicken broth
$\frac{1}{2}$ teaspoon salt
$\frac{1}{2}$ teaspoon pepper
1 tablespoon chopped fresh parsley
3 shredded carrots
$\frac{1}{2}$ cup sliced celery with leaves
1 8-ounce package tortellini (use half)*

Peel and cut ends off onion; insert whole cloves into the onion. In a large pot, combine onion, chicken, broth, salt, parsley, carrots, and celery. Bring to a boil, reduce heat. Simmer uncovered for $1\frac{1}{2}$ hours. Remove onion. Cool soup, put in container, and store in freezer.

To prepare for serving, thaw soup, put in large pot, and heat until bubbly. Add the half package tortellini, and boil 25 minutes more.

SUMMARY OF PROCESSES:

Chop cooked chicken; shred 3 carrots; slice $\frac{1}{2}$ cup celery; chop 1 tablespoon parsley.

FREEZE IN: 8-cup container
SERVE WITH: Sautéed Apples with Thyme; Erica's Oatmeal Cookies

Makes 4 servings

Meal-in-One Potatoes

$\frac{1}{2}$ pound ground turkey
$\frac{1}{2}$ cup finely chopped onion
1 teaspoon minced garlic
1 15-ounce can red kidney beans, drained
1 15-ounce can tomatoes diced, not drained
1 8-ounce can tomato sauce
$\frac{1}{2}$ cup chile sauce
1 teaspoon dried oregano leaves
$\frac{1}{4}$ teaspoon salt
4 medium baking potatoes*

In a medium skillet, cook ground turkey, onion, and garlic until turkey is browned, about 10 to 15 minutes; add remaining ingredients except potatoes. Bring to a boil; reduce heat. Simmer 5 minutes. Cool and freeze in a 1-quart bag.

To serve, thaw filling. Wash and prick potatoes and bake in a preheated 400°F oven for 1 hour or until done. Heat filling. Split tops of baked potatoes lengthwise and fluff pulp with a fork. Top each potato with filling.

SUMMARY OF PROCESSES:

Chop $\frac{1}{2}$ cup onion.

FREEZE IN: 1-quart bag
SERVE WITH: Roasted Corn on the Cob with Chili Butter

Makes 4 servings

Teriyaki Burgers

2 tablespoons teriyaki sauce (See recipe for marinade in the Asian Chicken recipe.)
1 pound lean ground beef
4 sandwich rolls*

Mix teriyaki sauce into ground beef and form four patties. Freeze patties in a 1-gallon freezer bag with a piece of waxed paper between each patty. Freeze sandwich rolls.

To serve, thaw rolls and patties. Grill or fry meat to desired pinkness. Serve on warmed sandwich rolls.

FREEZE IN: 1-gallon bag
SERVE WITH: Crudités; Barbie's White Chocolate Chip Macadamia Nut Cookies

Makes 3 to 4 servings

Bacon-Wrapped Meat Loaf

4 strips of bacon
1 pound lean ground beef
Salt
Lemon pepper
$\frac{1}{4}$ cup grated Parmesan cheese
2 ounces mushroom stems and pieces, drained
1 tablespoon minced onion
2 tablespoons finely chopped green bell pepper

In a small skillet or microwave, cook bacon until limp, about 10 minutes. Drain bacon on paper towel. Pat ground beef on waxed paper into a $12 \times 8 \times \frac{1}{4}$-inch rectangle. Sprinkle lightly with salt and lemon pepper. Top with Parmesan cheese.

Combine mushrooms, onion, and bell pepper and sprinkle evenly over ground beef. Roll ground beef like a jelly roll, starting from the longest side. Wrap with a strip of bacon, securing with wooden picks. Store in bag. Label and freeze.

To serve, thaw; place meat loaf in pan and cover. Bake one hour at 350°F. Let meat loaf rest before cutting. Cut each slice between strips of bacon.

SUMMARY OF PROCESSES:
Chop 2 tablespoons green bell pepper. Mince 1 tablespoon onion.

FREEZE IN: 1-gallon bag
SERVE WITH: Spicy Grilled Pineapple; baked beans

Makes 4 servings

Joes to Go

1 pound lean ground beef
$\frac{3}{4}$ cup finely chopped onion
$1\frac{1}{4}$ teaspoons garlic salt
$\frac{1}{8}$ teaspoon pepper
$\frac{1}{2}$ cup chile sauce
$\frac{1}{4}$ cup light brown sugar
1 tablespoon white vinegar
1 tablespoon prepared mustard
1 8-ounce can tomato sauce
6 hamburger buns*

In a large skillet, cook and stir ground beef and onion until beef is brown, about 15 minutes; drain. Add garlic salt, pepper, chili sauce, brown sugar, white vinegar, mustard, and tomato sauce. Bring to a boil; reduce heat. Simmer uncovered 10 minutes, stirring occasionally. Cool and freeze. Keep with hamburger buns.

To prepare for serving, thaw hamburger sauce and buns. Heat sauce until bubbly and serve on warmed buns. Makes enough for 6 buns.

SUMMARY OF PROCESSES:

Chop $\frac{3}{4}$ cup onion.

FREEZE IN: 8-cup container
SERVE WITH: Steamed Edamame; Watermelon Salad

Makes 6 servings

Ravioli Soup

    1   pound lean ground beef
    $\frac{1}{4}$ cup grated Parmesan cheese
    $\frac{3}{4}$ teaspoon onion salt
    1   teaspoon minced garlic
    1   tablespoon olive oil or vegetable oil
    $1\frac{1}{2}$ cups finely chopped onion
    1   28-ounce can Italian-style or plain crushed tomatoes in puree
    1   6-ounce can tomato paste
    1   $14\frac{1}{2}$-ounce can beef broth or bouillon
    1   cup water
    $\frac{1}{2}$ teaspoon sugar
    $\frac{1}{2}$ teaspoon dried basil leaves
    $\frac{1}{4}$ teaspoon dried thyme leaves
    $\frac{1}{4}$ teaspoon dried oregano leaves
    $\frac{1}{4}$ cup chopped fresh parsley
    1   13-ounce package plain ravioli without sauce*
Salt
Grated Parmesan cheese*

Cook the ground beef in a large pot until browned, about 15 minutes. Drain the fat. Combine remaining ingredients except frozen ravioli and additional Parmesan cheese. Bring soup to a boil; reduce heat. Cover and simmer 10 minutes, stirring occasionally. Cool, put in container, and freeze.

To prepare for serving, thaw soup and put in a large pot. Bring to a boil; reduce heat. Simmer uncovered for at least 30 minutes, stirring occasionally. Thaw and cook ravioli according to package directions until just tender. Drain ravioli; add to soup. Salt to taste. Serve with Parmesan cheese.

SUMMARY OF PROCESSES:
    Chop $1\frac{1}{2}$ cup onion, $\frac{1}{4}$ cup parsley.

    FREEZE IN: 10-cup container
    SERVE WITH: Green salad tossed with Vinaigrette; French bread

Makes 6 servings

Taco Pie

1¼ pounds lean ground beef
⅓ cup finely chopped onion
1 package taco seasoning mix
1 4-ounce can diced green chilies, drained
1 cup milk (whole, 2%, or skim)
1 cup biscuit baking mix
2 large eggs
1 cup grated mild Cheddar cheese
2 tomatoes, sliced*
8 ounces sour cream (or plain low-fat yogurt)*
1 chopped tomato*
Shredded lettuce (enough to garnish pie)*

In a large skillet, cook and stir ground beef and onion until beef is brown, about 20 minutes; drain. Combine beef with taco seasoning mix and spread in a 10-inch pie plate. Sprinkle with chilies. Beat milk, biscuit baking mix, and eggs until smooth, 15 seconds on high in a blender or 1 minute with hand beater. Pour milk mixture over beef in pie plate. Cover plate with foil and freeze. Store a 1-quart bag of grated cheese with pie.

To prepare for serving, thaw pie. Bake uncovered in a preheated 400°F oven for 35 minutes. Top with sliced tomatoes; sprinkle with cheese. Bake until golden brown, 8 to 10 minutes. Top with sour cream, chopped tomato, and shredded lettuce.

SUMMARY OF PROCESSES:

Chop ⅓ cup onion; grate 1 cup cheddar cheese.

FREEZE IN: 10-inch quiche or pie plate; 1-quart bag
SERVE WITH: Guacamole dip with tortilla chips; slices of seasonal fruit

Makes 6 to 8 servings

Baked Herb Fish Fillets

4 fish fillets (about 1¼ pounds orange roughy or sole)*
½ cup Italian-flavored bread crumbs
¼ cup grated Parmesan cheese
¼ teaspoon garlic powder
¼ teaspoon salt
1 large egg white, lightly beaten*
4 to 5 new potatoes*
1 small lemon*

Freeze fish fillets in a 1-gallon bag. Combine bread crumbs, Parmesan cheese, garlic powder, and salt in a 1-quart bag; attach to fish fillet package.

To prepare to serve, thaw fish and bread crumb mixture. Lightly beat egg white and dip fillets in it. Put fillets one at a time in bag with bread crumb mixture; make sure each is coated. Remove and arrange fillets in baking dish. Bake in preheated 375°F oven for about 15 minutes (until fish flakes easily) or in a microwave oven on high for 4 to 5 minutes.

At the same time, prepare new potatoes. Peel a strip around the center of each potato. Heat 1 cup salted water to a boil; add potatoes. Cover, heat until boiling; reduce heat.

Simmer tightly covered until tender, 30 to 35 minutes; drain. Serve potatoes with fish and lemon wedges.

FREEZE IN: 1-gallon bag; 1-quart bag
SERVE WITH: Roasted Grape Tomatoes; Italian Parsley Salad

Makes 4 servings

Aztec Quiche

$1\frac{1}{4}$ cups grated Monterey Jack cheese
$\frac{3}{4}$ cup grated mild Cheddar cheese
1 9-inch, deep-dish frozen pie shell
1 4-ounce can diced green chilies
1 cup half-and-half
3 large eggs, beaten lightly
$\frac{1}{2}$ teaspoon salt
$\frac{1}{8}$ teaspoon ground cumin

Spread Monterey Jack cheese and half of Cheddar over bottom of pie shell. Sprinkle diced chilies over cheeses. In a bowl mix the half-and-half, eggs, and seasonings. Pour carefully into pie shell. Sprinkle with remaining Cheddar. Cover pie with foil and freeze.

To prepare for serving, thaw pie and remove foil. Bake uncovered in a preheated 325°F oven for 40 to 50 minutes.

SUMMARY OF PROCESSES:

Grate $1\frac{1}{4}$ cups Monterey Jack cheese and $\frac{3}{4}$ cup mild Cheddar cheese.

FREEZE IN: 9-inch, oven-proof quiche or pie pan
SERVE WITH: Mango and Avocado (sliced, arranged on a plate, and sprinkled with lemon juice)

Add salt and pepper if desired.
Wonderful to serve for a wedding reception. Quiches can be made in advance.

Makes 6 to 8 servings

Mustard Barbecued Chicken

$\frac{1}{2}$ cup Dijon mustard
3 tablespoons white vinegar
4 teaspoons Worchestershire sauce
1 teaspoon thyme
3 pounds chicken legs and thighs

Stir together mustard, vinegar, Worcestershire sauce, and thyme in a gallon freezer bag. Pull skin from chicken pieces. Rinse and pat dry, and put into the bag. Label and freeze.

To serve, thaw chicken in marinade. Drain, reserving marinade. Grill chicken bone-side down over a drip pan surrounded by medium-hot coals. Cover and grill 40–50 minutes or until no longer pink inside, brushing occasionally with remaining marinade. Discard unused marinade.

SUMMARY OF PROCESSES:

Pull skin from chicken pieces.

FREEZE IN: One gallon freezer bag
SERVE WITH: Cucumber salad and new potatoes

Makes 6 servings

Brined Salmon Fillet

1 1½-pound salmon fillet

BRINE

½ cup kosher salt
¼ cup sugar
2 tablespoons dill weed (dried)
2 tablespoons soy sauce

Place Brine ingredients in quart bag, seal and tape to the container that holds the fish. Freeze. When needed, thaw salmon and place in 13×9-inch pan. One hour before meal, mix salt ingredients with 3½ cups water and pour over salmon. Make sure the whole fish is under brine. Float 1 cup of ice cubes over fish. Turn once. Then remove fish, wash under cool water, and barbeque until done.

> **FREEZE IN:** Leave salmon in store packaging. Tape 1-quart bag brine onto the container.
> **SERVE WITH:** Spicy Grilled Pineapple; Watermelon Salad

Makes 4 servings

Slow Cooker Fall Pork Roast

1 2-pound pork tenderloin
3 cups apple juice
1 16-ounce can whole berry cranberry sauce
$\frac{3}{4}$ teaspoon salt
$\frac{1}{2}$ teaspoon pepper

Place all ingredients in 1-gallon Ziploc bag. Label and freeze.

To cook, thaw, place all ingredients in slow cooker and cover. Cook 6 to 8 hours on low.

FREEZE IN: 1-gallon bag
SERVE WITH: Twice-Baked Sweet Potatoes

Makes 6 servings

London Broil in Marinade

2 pounds London broil

MARINADE

1 cup soy sauce
$\frac{1}{2}$ cup orange juice
$\frac{1}{2}$ cup light brown sugar
$\frac{1}{2}$ cup white vinegar
1 teaspoon minced garlic

Place London broil in 1-gallon bag.
Mix marinade in small bowl and add it to meat bag. Label and freeze.
When ready to serve, remove meat and pour marinade into small saucepan.
Boil marinade.
Grill meat over medium-hot coals until desired doneness. Use marinade for basting. Depending on the thickness of the meat, this could take up to one hour.

FREEZE IN: 1-gallon bag
SERVE WITH: Baked potatoes; Gingered Carrots

Makes 4 servings

Slow Cooker Beer Corned Beef

1 3-pound cured corned beef brisket

MARINADE
  1 cup chopped onion
  1 cup chopped carrot
  1 cup chopped celery
  $\frac{2}{3}$ cup light brown sugar
  $\frac{1}{2}$ cup catsup
  1 tablespoon dried dill
  6 black peppercorns
  2 whole cloves
  1 14$\frac{1}{2}$-ounce can beef broth*
  1 12-ounce bottle stout beer*

Remove brisket from packaging and wash until all spices are removed. Place in 1-gallon Ziploc bag. To meat bag add veggie with spices bag. Label and freeze. When desired: Thaw and place meat into slow cooker, add ingredients from veggie bag and pour beef broth and beer over all. Cook on high for 8 hours or until meat is tender. Remove beef and cut diagonally.

SUMMARY OF PROCESSES:
  Wash corned beef; chop 1 cup onion; chop 1 cup carrots; chop 1 cup celery.

  FREEZE IN: 1-quart bag; 1-gallon bag
  SERVE WITH: Broiled cabbage, potatoes and carrots. Pass the mustard.

Makes 6 servings

Slow Cooker Beef Goulash

2 pounds beef stew meat cut into bite-size pieces
2 cups chopped onion
1 cup chopped carrots
1 cup chopped red bell pepper (1 medium)
$\frac{1}{3}$ cup catsup
1 tablespoon Worcestershire sauce
2 teaspoons paprika
2 teaspoons minced garlic
1 teaspoon salt
1 14$\frac{1}{2}$-ounce can beef broth

Place all ingredients in a 1-gallon plastic bag. Label and freeze.

To cook, thaw and place ingredients from bag in slow cooker, cover, and cook on low for 8 hours.

SUMMARY OF PROCESSES:

Cut stew meat into bite-size pieces; chop 1 cup onion; chop 1 cup carrots; chop 1 cup red bell pepper.

FREEZE IN: 1-gallon bag
SERVE WITH: Mashed potatoes and green beans

Makes 6 servings

6

One-Month Entrée Plan E

Grocery Shopping and Staples Lists

An asterisk (*) after an item indicates that it should be stored until the day you cook the dish with which it is served. Mark those items with an "X" as a reminder that you will need them for an entrée.

When entrées require perishable foods to be refrigerated until served, you may want to prepare those dishes right away or buy the food the week you plan to make the dish. For example, fresh mushrooms would spoil by the end of a month.

For this one-month entrée plan, you will need these food items as well as the ones in the staples list that follows.

GROCERY SHOPPING LIST

CANNED GOODS

1 bottle barbecue sauce*
1 $10\frac{3}{4}$-ounce can beef consommé
1 8-ounce bottle chili sauce
1 $10\frac{3}{4}$-ounce can condensed cream of chicken soup
3 $10\frac{3}{4}$-ounce cans condensed cream of mushroom soup
1 small jar orange marmalade
3 4-ounce cans diced green chilies
1 16-ounce can whole green beans
1 16-ounce can Great Northern beans
2 15-ounce cans kidney beans
1 16-ounce can small peas
1 8-ounce and 1 4-ounce can mushroom stems and pieces
1 4-ounce jar pimientos
1 28-ounce can pork and beans
2 8-ounce cans pineapple chunks*
1 10-ounce bottle soy sauce
2 14.5-ounce cans peeled tomatoes
2 6-ounce cans tomato paste
1 15-ounce can and 2 8-ounce cans tomato sauce
1 12-ounce can tomato juice
1 8-ounce can sliced water chestnuts
1 15-ounce can pinto beans
3 cups V8 juice
4 14.5-ounce cans chicken broth
1 15-ounce can cannellini beans
1 $14\frac{1}{2}$-ounce can Italian-style stewed tomatoes
1 cup cranberry juice
1 small jar Dijon mustard
1 16-ounce can whole berry cranberry sauce
1 16-ounce jar salsa verde
1 16-ounce jar salsa
1 4.5-ounce jar crushed garlic

GRAINS, PASTA, AND RICE

8 sandwich or onion rolls*

4 hamburger buns*

1 package hot dog buns*

1 5-ounce can chow mein noodles*

1 12-ounce package wide egg noodles

12 ounces dried green split peas

1 32-ounce and 1 16-ounce package regular rice

1 16-ounce package spaghetti

8 to 12 flour tortillas

DRY INGREDIENTS AND SEASONINGS

1 1.25-ounce envelope onion soup mix

1 package French's or Good Seasons French Dip, or brown gravy mix*

Soda crackers (for $\frac{1}{2}$ cup crumbs)

1 $1\frac{1}{4}$-ounce package taco seasoning

1 9-inch refrigerated pie crust

Tortilla chips (optional)*

Dry bread crumbs

Croutons

FROZEN FOODS

1 10-ounce package frozen, chopped spinach

1 package puff pastry shells*

1 16-ounce package frozen small onions

DAIRY PRODUCTS

$\frac{1}{2}$ cup sweet, unsalted butter (1 stick, or 4 ounces)

16 large eggs*

4 8-ounce containers sour cream

20 ounces grated mild Cheddar cheese

24 ounces Monterey Jack cheese, grated

4 slices Monterey Jack cheese

20 ounces mozzarella cheese, grated

8 ounces shredded mozzarella cheese

8 ounces grated Parmesan cheese

2 16-ounce cartons Ricotta cheese

1 cup half-and-half

1 pint milk (whole, 2%, or skim)

16 ounces cottage cheese

MEAT, POULTRY, AND FISH

   2 pounds boneless, cubed top sirloin steak
   12 pounds lean ground beef
   1⅓ pounds flank steak
   2 pounds round steak
   3 to 4 pounds sirloin tip or boneless beef rump roast
   3 pounds beef stew meat
   12 pounds boneless, skinless chicken breasts (2 pounds can be boneless
      thighs if you prefer)
   4 strips bacon
   6 pounds cooked ham (½ pound cubed, ½ pound sliced thin, 2 pounds from
      the center portion cut in thick dinner slices, and 1 3-pound whole
      ham*)
   2 pounds bulk Italian pork or turkey sausage
   1 3-to-4-pound pork loin
   1 pound lasagna
   Salmon (enough for the family)
   1 package beef franks*

PRODUCE

   7 carrots
   1 bunch celery
   2 bunches green onions
   4 green bell peppers
   4 ounces whole fresh mushrooms*
   10 yellow onions
   1 half-pint box cherry tomatoes*
   1 bunch parsley

STAPLES LIST

   Make sure you have the following staples on hand; add those you don't have to
your shopping list.

   basil leaves, dried
   bay leaves
   bread (1 slice)
   catsup (½ cup)
   chili powder
   cinnamon, ground

cloves, ground

cornstarch

cumin

dill weed

dry mustard

fennel seeds

flour, all-purpose (about $\frac{3}{4}$ cup)

ginger, ground

lemon juice ($\frac{1}{3}$ cup)

light brown sugar ($1\frac{1}{8}$ cups)

minute tapioca ($\frac{1}{4}$ cup)

nonstick spray

onion powder

onion salt

oregano, dried

paprika

parsley flakes

pepper

prepared mustard

red pepper flakes

red wine ($1\frac{1}{2}$ cups)

salt

seasoned salt

sherry

sugar

thyme leaves, dried

vegetable oil

white vinegar ($\frac{1}{2}$ cup)

white wine ($1\frac{1}{4}$ cups)

Worcestershire sauce

Freezer Containers

The following list of freezer containers or baking dishes will be needed for the entrées. These are not the only containers you can use, but this list gives you an idea of the size and number of containers you'll need. Labeling containers before you cook works best.

One-Month Entrée Plan E

SUN.	MON.	TUES.	WED.	THURS.	FRI.	SAT.
	1 Eat Out Cooking Day!	2 Split Pea Soup	3 Chili Dogs	4 Jack Burgers	5 Deborah's Sweet-and-Sour Chicken	6 French Stew
7 Shish Kebabs	8 Chicken and Rice Pilaf	9 Grandma's Chili	10 Crustless Spinach Quiche	11 Grilled Ham Slices	12 Green Chile Enchiladas	13 Chicken à la King
14 Slow Cooker Cranberry Pork	15 Oriental Chicken	16 Marinated Flank Steak	17 Three-Bean Taco Chili	18 Sicilian Meat Roll	19 Dawn's Lasagna	20 Italian Shepherd's Pie
21 Southwestern Chicken Soup	22 Rosie's Meat Loaf	23 Baked Beans and Hamburger	24 Glazed Ham	25 Bird's Nest Pie	26 Chicken Tetrazzini	27 French Dip
28 Lemon Chicken	29 Grilled Salmon	30 Mexican Stroganoff				

Waxed paper: Sicilian Meat Roll, Jack Burgers
Heavy-Duty Aluminum Foil: French Dip

6 1-quart freezer bags: Green Chili Enchiladas (1); Bird's Nest Pie (1); Grilled Salmon (1); Crustless Spinach Quiche (1); Slow Cooker Cranberry Pork (1); Chili Dogs (1)

11 1-gallon freezer bags: Grilled Ham Slices (1); Jack Burgers (1); Lemon Chicken (1); Chicken à la King (1); Oriental Chicken (1); Marinated Flank Steak (1); Sicilian Meat Roll (1); Slow Cooker Cranberry Pork (1); Rosie's Meat Loaf (1); Glazed Ham (1); French Dip (1)

2 3-cup containers: Grandma's Chili; Chili Dogs

6 6-cup containers: Split Pea Soup (1); Chicken Tetrazzini (2); Shish Kebabs (1); Mexican Stroganoff (1); Baked Beans and Hamburger (1)

2 8-cup containers: Deborah's Sweet and Sour Chicken; Southwestern Chicken Soup

1 12-cup container: Three-Bean Taco Chili

1 14-cup container: French Stew

2 $11 \times 7 \times 1\frac{1}{2}$-inch baking dishes: Chicken and Rice Pilaf; Bird's Nest Pie

3 $13 \times 9 \times 2$-inch baking dishes: Dawn's Lasagna; Green Chili Enchiladas

3 10-inch quiche or pie plates: Crustless Spinach Quiche; Bird's Nest Pie; Italian Shepherd's Pie

The Day Before Cooking Day

1. Put away all the items you've purchased that won't be used until the day the entrées are eaten.
2. Put frozen spinach for Easy Ravioli Lasagna in a pan in the refrigerator to thaw.
3. In 2 $13 \times 9 \times 2$-inch casserole dishes cook 8 pounds of boneless, skinless chicken breasts, covered, at 375°F for 50 minutes. When cooled, dice all the chicken and store sealed in bags in the refrigerator.
4. Set out appliances, bowls, canned goods, dry ingredients, freezer containers, and recipes.
5. Rinse split peas, and soak them covered with cold water overnight.
6. Start French Stew in Crock-Pot (just before bed).

On Cooking Day, Before Assembling Dishes

1. Make sure you've cleared the table and counters of unnecessary kitchenware to allow plenty of working room. It also helps to have fresh, damp washcloths and towels for wiping your hands and the cooking area. The day will go a lot smoother if you clean and organize as you work.
2. Before you prepare a recipe, gather all the spices and ingredients in the assembly area to save time and steps. When you finish the recipe, remove unneeded items, and wipe off the work space.
3. Perform all chopping, crushing, grating, and slicing tasks.
     Green onions: Chop 9.
     Green bell peppers: Chop 4; save 1 whole in refrigerator.*
     Celery: Slice $1\frac{1}{3}$ cups.
     Carrots: Peel and slice 5 carrots.
     Crumbs: Crush $\frac{1}{2}$ cup soda cracker crumbs and $\frac{1}{4}$ cup crouton crumbs.
     Onions: Chop 8 fine; chop 1 coarsely; save 1 whole.*
     Bacon: Dice 3 strips (kitchen scissors work best).
     Ham: Cube $\frac{1}{2}$ pound and cut 2 pounds into 2 thick slices ($\frac{3}{4}$-inch thick).
     Sirloin steak: Cube.
     Round steak: Cut into bite-size pieces.

Assembly Order

ASSEMBLE BEEF DISHES

1. Cool and freeze French Stew.
2. Brown $4\frac{1}{4}$ pounds of ground beef in a large Dutch oven with four cups of chopped onions. This mixture will be measured and used for the next three recipes.
3. Assemble and freeze Green Chile Enchiladas.
4. Assemble and freeze Baked Beans and Hamburger.
5. Start Grandma's Chili in the Crock-Pot.
6. Assemble and freeze French Dip.
7. Assemble and freeze Marinated Flank Steak.
8. Assemble and freeze Shish Kebabs.
9. Assemble and freeze Rosie's Meat loaf.
10. Assemble and freeze Jack Burgers.
11. Assemble and freeze Sicilian Meat Roll.

12. Prepare and freeze Mexican Stroganoff.
13. Prepare and freeze Three-Bean Taco Chili.

ASSEMBLE MISCELLANEOUS AND FISH DISHES

1. Prepare and freeze Dawn's Lasagna.
2. Assemble and freeze Grilled Salmon.
3. Assemble and freeze Crustless Spinach Quiche.

ASSEMBLE PORK DISHES

1. Start browning 2 pounds Italian bulk sausage for the Bird's Nest Pie and the Italian Shepherd's Pie.
2. Cook a 16-ounce package spaghetti, half for Bird's Nest Pie and half for Chicken Tetrazzini.
3. Assemble and freeze Slow Cooker Cranberry Pork.
4. Start cooking split Pea Soup.
5. Assemble and freeze Italian Shepherd's Pie.
6. Assemble and freeze Bird's Nest Pie.
7. Assemble and freeze Grilled Ham.
8. Assemble and freeze Glazed Ham.
9. Cool and freeze Grandma's Chili and Chili Dogs.

ASSEMBLE CHICKEN DISHES

1. Assemble and freeze Chicken Tetrazzini.
2. Assemble and freeze Deborah's Sweet and Sour Chicken.
3. Assemble and freeze Chicken à la King.
4. Assemble and freeze Southwestern Chicken Soup.
5. Assemble and freeze Lemon Chicken.
6. Assemble and freeze Chicken and Rice Pilaf.
7. Assemble and freeze Oriental Chicken.

Recipes for the One-Month Entrée Plan E

Each recipe offers complete instructions on how to prepare the dish. Food items with an asterisk (*) won't be prepared until you serve the entrée. For recipes calling for oven baking, preheat oven for about 10 minutes.

"Summary of processes" gives a quick overview of foods that need to be chopped, diced, grated, or sliced. "Freeze in" tells what bags and containers will be needed to freeze each entrée. "Serve with" offers suggestions of foods to accompany the meal. Some of the recipes for those foods are included in chapter 8; page numbers are indicated for easy reference. "Note" includes special instructions on how the entrée can be used in other ways.

French Stew

3 pounds beef stew meat
1 $10\frac{3}{4}$-ounce can beef consommé
3 large peeled and sliced carrots
1 16-ounce can whole green beans, drained
8 ounces frozen small onions, separated
1 16-ounce can small peas, drained
1 16-ounce can peeled tomatoes
1 cup white wine
$\frac{1}{4}$ cup minute tapioca
1 tablespoon brown sugar
$\frac{1}{2}$ cup fine, dry bread crumbs
1 bay leaf
1 tablespoon salt or to taste
$\frac{1}{4}$ teaspoon pepper

Mix all the ingredients and bake in Crock-Pot, 8 to 10 hours on low. Allow to cool, and freeze.

To prepare for serving, thaw stew and heat until bubbly in a large pot about 30 minutes.

SUMMARY OF PROCESSES:
Peel and slice 3 carrots.

FREEZE IN: 14-cup container
SERVE WITH: Tossed green salad with Creamy Dressing; French bread

Makes 8 servings

Green Chile Enchiladas

$1\frac{1}{2}$ pounds lean ground beef
$1\frac{1}{4}$ cups finely chopped onion
 1 tablespoon chili powder
 1 teaspoon cumin
Salt and pepper to taste
 2 cups grated Monterey Jack cheese (1 cup*)
 8 to 12 flour tortillas
 1 $10\frac{3}{4}$-ounce can condensed cream of chicken soup
$\frac{1}{2}$ cup milk
$1\frac{1}{2}$ cups sour cream
 1 4-ounce can diced, green chilies

Cook the ground beef, and sauté onions until the meat is brown, about 15 minutes. Drain the fat. Combine with chili powder, cumin, salt and pepper. Reserve 1 cup cheese in a 1-quart freezer bag to use when serving. Spoon enough meat mixture and cheese on each tortilla to cover a third of it. Roll tortilla beginning at the filled edge. Place seam side down in a 13×9×2-inch baking dish treated with nonstick spray. When tortillas are completed, combine soup, sour cream, milk, and green chilies to make a sauce; pour over tortillas. Cover dish with foil and freeze with bag of cheese taped to it.

To prepare for serving, thaw enchiladas and cheese. Bake uncovered in a preheated 375°F oven for 20 to 25 minutes. In the last 10 minutes sprinkle the remaining cheese on top.

SUMMARY OF PROCESSES:
    Chop $1\frac{1}{4}$ cups onion.

    FREEZE IN: 13×9×2-inch baking dish
    SERVE WITH: Shredded lettuce, chopped tomato, and avocados

Makes 8 servings

Baked Beans and Hamburger

3 strips bacon, diced
$\frac{3}{4}$ pound lean ground beef
$1\frac{1}{4}$ cups finely chopped onions
1 28-ounce can pork and beans in tomato sauce
1 8-ounce can tomato sauce
$\frac{1}{4}$ cup brown sugar
1 tablespoon prepared mustard
$\frac{1}{4}$ cup catsup
Salt and pepper to taste

Cook bacon; drain on a paper towel, let cool, then dice. In a large skillet, cook the ground beef and sauté onions until tender, about 15 minutes. Drain the fat. Mix in bacon and remaining ingredients, put in container, and freeze.

To prepare for serving, thaw and bake uncovered in a large baking dish in preheated 350°F oven for 30 to 45 minutes.

SUMMARY OF PROCESSES:

Cook, then dice 3 strips bacon; chop $1\frac{1}{4}$ cups onions.

FREEZE IN: 6-cup container
SERVE WITH: Corn on the cob; tossed green salad

Makes 6 servings

Grandma's Chili

2 pounds lean ground beef
1½ cups finely chopped onion
1 cup chopped green bell pepper
1 tablespoon Worcestershire sauce
¾ teaspoon chili powder
¼ teaspoon ground cinnamon
½ teaspoon crushed garlic
Salt and black pepper to taste
1 15-ounce can kidney beans, drained
1 16-ounce can peeled tomatoes
1 6-ounce can tomato paste
1 15-ounce can tomato sauce

Cook the ground beef with onions in a large saucepan until brown, about 20 minutes. Drain the fat and add remaining ingredients. Bring to a boil; reduce heat. Cover and simmer over low heat for 2 hours on a back burner or in a Crock-Pot on low for 6 hours, stirring occasionally. Cool and freeze in 3 cup container.

To serve chili, thaw and heat in saucepan until hot and bubbly, about 30 minutes.

SUMMARY OF PROCESSES:

Chop 1½ cups onion, 1 cup green bell pepper.

FREEZE IN: 3-cup container for Grandma's Chili; 3-cup container for Chili Dogs.
SERVE WITH: Multigrain rolls; cottage cheese with pineapple chunks and mandarin orange slices

Makes 4 servings

French Dip

3 to 4 pounds sirloin tip or boneless beef rump roast
Worcestershire sauce
8 sandwich rolls*
1 packet French's or Food Seasons French Dip, or brown gravy mix*

Douse roast with Worcestershire sauce; seal meat in bag and freeze.
When thawed, put the roast in the Crock-Pot and sprinkle the dip or gravy mix on top. Cook for 6 to 8 hours on low. Allow roast to sit 20 minutes before slicing.
Serve thin slices of roast in sandwich rolls with bowls of juice for dipping.

FREEZE IN: 1-gallon bag
SERVE WITH: Waldorf salad; carrot strips

Makes 6 to 8 servings

Marinated Flank Steak

$1\frac{1}{3}$ pounds flank steak

MARINADE

$\frac{1}{2}$ cup vegetable oil

$\frac{1}{2}$ cup soy sauce

$\frac{1}{4}$ cup sherry

2 teaspoons Worcestershire sauce

$\frac{1}{2}$ teaspoon ground ginger

$\frac{1}{2}$ teaspoon crushed garlic

Mix ingredients for Marinade. Put flank steak in a freezer bag, pour marinade over it, seal bag, and freeze.

To prepare for serving, thaw flank steak, remove from marinade, and barbecue 8 to 10 minutes per side; or set oven control to broil and/or 550°F. Broil steak 6 inches from heat until brown, turning once, about 6 minutes on one side and 4 minutes on the other. Cut steak across grain at slanted angle into thin slices.

FREEZE IN: 1-gallon bag
SERVE WITH: Cauliflower Mock Potato Salad

Makes 4 servings

Shish Kebabs

  2 pounds cubed, boneless, top sirloin steak
  $\frac{3}{4}$ cup coarsely chopped onion
  1 4-ounce can diced green chiles
$1\frac{1}{4}$ teaspoons chili powder
  1 tablespoon vegetable oil
  $\frac{1}{4}$ cup dry red wine
  $\frac{1}{4}$ teaspoon salt
Pepper
  $\frac{1}{2}$ green bell pepper*
  1 onion*
  4 ounces whole fresh mushrooms*
  1 half-pint box cherry tomatoes*
  $\frac{1}{2}$ of 1 8-ounce can pineapple chunks*
  1 cup regular, uncooked rice*

Combine cubed beef with chopped onion, salsa, chili powder, vegetable oil, red wine, salt, and pepper; put in a 6-cup container and freeze.

To prepare for serving, thaw meat mixture. Remove meat from marinade. Cut bell pepper and onion into thick pieces to put on a skewer. Alternate meat, vegetables, tomatoes, and pineapple on a skewer, and barbecue or broil. Baste with marinade while cooking. At the same time, prepare rice according to package directions. Serve Shish Kebabs with rice.

SUMMARY OF PROCESSES:

Cut steak into cubes; chop $\frac{3}{4}$ cup onion into thick pieces.

FREEZE IN: 6-cup container
SERVE WITH: Corn on the cob; Erica's Oatmeal White Chocolate Cookies
NOTE: Serve these the first week; otherwise, fresh vegetables will spoil.

Makes 4 servings

Rosie's Meat Loaf

- 2 pounds ground beef
- 2 large eggs
- $\frac{1}{2}$ cup cracker crumbs (or stuffing)
- $\frac{1}{3}$ cup green bell pepper
- $\frac{1}{4}$ cup milk
- $\frac{1}{4}$ cup catsup
- $1\frac{1}{4}$ teaspoon salt
- $\frac{1}{8}$ teaspoon pepper
- $\frac{3}{4}$ cup onion, chopped
- 1 cup barbecue sauce*

Mix all ingredients but barbecue sauce together in a medium-size mixing bowl (hands work best). Place meat loaf in freezer bag, then shape, in bag, to fit a loaf pan. Freeze.

When thawed, pour on barbecue sauce and bake $1\frac{1}{4}$ hours at 350°F.

SUMMARY OF PROCESSES:

Crush $\frac{1}{2}$ cup cracker crumbs; chop $\frac{1}{3}$ cup green pepper; $\frac{3}{4}$ cup chopped onion

FREEZE IN: 1-gallon freezer bag
SERVE WITH: Twice-baked Sweet Potatoes; broccoli

Makes 6 to 8 servings

Jack Burgers

$1\frac{1}{4}$ pounds lean ground beef
$\frac{1}{2}$ teaspoon onion salt
$\frac{1}{4}$ teaspoon freshly ground black pepper
4 thin slices Monterey Jack cheese
4 hamburger buns*

Form ground beef into 8 thin patties. Sprinkle onion salt and black pepper over them. Place a slice of cheese on 4 of the patties. Cover each with another patty, pinching to seal cheese inside. Freeze in a 1-gallon freezer bag with waxed paper between each set of patties.

To serve, thaw patties and buns; grill or fry to desired doneness.

FREEZE IN: 1-gallon bag
SERVE WITH: Greek Pasta Salad

Makes 4 servings

Sicilian Meat Roll

2 slightly beaten large eggs

$\frac{3}{4}$ cup soft bread crumbs (1 slice)

$\frac{1}{2}$ cup tomato juice

2 tablespoons chopped parsley

$\frac{1}{2}$ teaspoon dried oregano, crushed

$\frac{1}{4}$ teaspoon salt

$\frac{1}{4}$ teaspoon pepper

$\frac{1}{2}$ teaspoon crushed garlic

2 pounds lean ground beef

8 1-ounce thin slices fully cooked ham

$1\frac{3}{4}$ cups shredded mozzarella cheese

In a large bowl combine eggs, bread crumbs, tomato juice, parsley, oregano, salt, pepper, and garlic. Stir in the ground beef, mixing well. On waxed paper, pat meat mixture into a 12×10-inch rectangle. Arrange ham slices atop meat, leaving a $\frac{3}{4}$-inch border around all edges. Sprinkle $1\frac{1}{2}$ cups of the shredded mozzarella cheese over ham. Starting from a short end, carefully roll up meat, using waxed paper to lift; seal edges and ends. Seal in a 1-gallon freezer bag, label and freeze.

When thawed, place roll, seam side down, in a 13×9×2-inch baking pan. Bake in a 350°F oven for 1 hour and 15 minutes or until a meat thermometer registers 170°F and juices run clear. (Center of meat roll will be pink because of the ham.) Sprinkle remaining shredded mozzarella over top of roll. Return to the oven for 5 minutes or until cheese melts.

SUMMARY OF PROCESSES:

Tear one slice soft white bread into crumbs; slice thinly 6 ounces ham.

FREEZE IN: 1-gallon bag

SERVE WITH: Eggplant sautéed with zucchini, tossed green salad with Creamy Dressing

Makes 8 to 10 servings

Mexican Stroganoff

2 pounds round steak
1 cup finely chopped onion
1 teaspoons crushed garlic
2 tablespoons vegetable oil
$1\frac{1}{4}$ cups red wine
$\frac{1}{2}$ cup water
$\frac{1}{2}$ cup chile sauce
1 tablespoon paprika
1 tablespoon chili powder
2 teaspoons seasoned salt
1 teaspoon soy sauce
1 8-ounce can mushroom stems and pieces, drained
1 12-ounce package wide egg noodles*
8 ounces sour cream*
3 tablespoons all-purpose flour*

Cut steak into bite-size pieces. Cook and stir steak, onion, and garlic in oil in a large saucepan over medium heat until brown, about 15 to 20 minutes. Drain oil. Stir wine, water, chile sauce, paprika, chili powder, seasoned salt, soy sauce, and mushrooms into steak mixture. Bring to a boil; reduce heat. Cover and simmer 1 hour until meat is tender. Cool and store in freezer container.

To prepare for serving, thaw meat mixture and heat in saucepan until bubbly. Cook egg noodles according to package directions. Stir sour cream or plain low-fat yogurt and flour together; combine with meat mixture to make a stroganoff. Heat to a boil, stirring constantly. Reduce heat; simmer and stir about 1 minute. Serve Stroganoff over noodles.

SUMMARY OF PROCESSES:

Chop 1 cup onion.

FREEZE IN: 6-cup container
SERVE WITH: Tomatoes Caprese

Makes 6 to 8 servings

Three-Bean Taco Chili

2 pounds ground beef
3 cups V8 juice
1 16-ounce jar salsa
1 15-ounce can kidney beans, drained and rinsed
1 16-ounce can pinto beans, drained and rinsed
1 16-ounce can Great Northern beans, drained and rinsed
1 8-ounce can tomato sauce
1 6-ounce can tomato paste
1 4-ounce can chopped green chilies
1 1¼-ounce package taco seasoning

In large pot, brown ground beef and drain off fat. Stir in remaining ingredients and bring to a boil. Reduce heat; simmer, uncovered for 15 minutes, stirring occasionally. Yields 12 cups.

FREEZE IN: 12-cup container
SERVE WITH: Bed of corn chips; Spicy Grilled Pineapple

Makes 10 to 12 servings

Dawn's Lasagna

1   26-ounce jar of pasta sauce (your favorite)
$\frac{3}{4}$ cup water
2   16-ounce cartons Ricotta cheese
3   eggs
1   teaspoon salt
$\frac{1}{2}$ teaspoon pepper
$\frac{2}{3}$ cup grated Parmesan cheese
1   16-ounce package shredded mozzarella cheese (divided)
4   tablespoons finely chopped parsley
1   pound lasagna

Prepare 13×9×2-inch casserole dish with cooking spray. Mix jar of pasta sauce with water. In another bowl mix Ricotta cheese, eggs, salt, pepper, Parmesan cheese, 8 ounces shredded mozzarella cheese, and the parsley.

Pour $\frac{1}{3}$ pasta sauce in prepared pan. Cover sauce with one layer of uncooked lasagna. Spread cheese mixture over the lasagna. Top with remaining lasagna, and finally with remaining pasta sauce, being careful to cover the lasagna.

Cover with heavy foil. Store remaining 8 ounces shredded mozzarella cheese in a quart bag taped to the dish, label, and freeze.

To serve, thaw lasagna and bake uncovered at 350°F for 45 minutes. Sprinkle with remaining shredded mozzarella and bake 10 more minutes.

FREEZE IN: 13×9×2-inch baking dish
SERVE WITH: Caesar salad and Asparagus Italiano

Makes 8 servings

Grilled Salmon

Salmon fillets
1 lemon*
Dill weed or fresh dill*
Paprika

Freeze thick salmon fillets in individual servings in 1-quart freezer bags. When thawed, place on foil that has been sprayed with nonstick spray, skin side down. Put a few lemon slices along top. Wrap in foil and grill (with cover on grill) about 20 minutes. Sprinkle with dill and paprika.

FREEZE IN: 1-quart freezer bags
SERVE WITH: Greek Pasta Salad

Makes 4 servings

Crustless Spinach Quiche

  1 10-ounce package frozen, chopped spinach
  1 bunch chopped green onions (white bulbs only)
  4 large eggs
16 ounces low-fat cottage cheese
  2 cups grated, mild Cheddar cheese
  $\frac{1}{4}$ cup crouton crumbs*

Thaw spinach to remove liquid. Combine spinach, green onion bulbs, eggs, cottage cheese, and cheddar cheese. Put into a quiche pan or 10-inch pie plate treated with nonstick spray. Cover with foil and freeze. Put crouton crumbs in a 1-quart bag and tape to pie plate.

To prepare for serving, thaw pie and crumbs. Bake uncovered in a preheated 325°F oven for 1 hour, adding crouton crumbs the last 15 minutes.

SUMMARY OF PROCESSES:

Chop 1 bunch green onion bulbs; crush croutons to make $\frac{1}{4}$ cup.

FREEZE IN: 10-inch quiche pan or pie plate; 1-quart bag
SERVE WITH: Fresh sliced tomatoes
NOTE: This dish is nice for a women's luncheon.

Makes 8 servings

Slow Cooker Cranberry Pork

1 pork loin, 3 to 4 pounds
2 tablespoons vegetable oil
1 16-ounce can whole berry cranberry sauce
$\frac{3}{4}$ cup sugar
1 cup cranberry juice
1 teaspoon dry mustard
1 teaspoon pepper
$\frac{1}{4}$ teaspoon ground cloves
2 tablespoons cornstarch*
$\frac{1}{2}$ cup cold water
Salt to taste

Brown roast in Dutch oven over medium-high heat. Freeze pork loin. Combine all ingredients but the last three and freeze in small freezer bag taped to the pork loin bag.

When thawed, mix together all ingredients and pour over roast. Cover and cook on low for 4 to 6 hours or until a meat thermometer reads 160°F. Remove roast and keep warm.

In a saucepan, combine cornstarch, cold water, and salt until smooth; stir in cooking juices. Bring to a boil; cook and stir for 2 minutes or till thickened. Serve with roast.

FREEZE IN: 1-quart freezer bag; 1-gallon freezer bag
SERVE WITH: Sweet potatoes

Makes 6 to 8 servings

Split Pea Soup

12 ounces dried green split peas
 3 cups water
 $\frac{1}{2}$ pound cooked, cubed ham
 $\frac{3}{4}$ teaspoon onion powder
 $\frac{1}{4}$ teaspoon dried thyme leaves
 $\frac{1}{4}$ teaspoon freshly ground pepper
 $\frac{1}{3}$ cup chopped celery
 $\frac{3}{4}$ cup peeled and sliced carrots
 1 cup finely chopped onion
 1 bay leaf
Salt to taste

Rinse split peas, soak them in cold water overnight; drain. Put peas with remaining ingredients in a large pot. Bring to a boil; reduce heat. Stirring occasionally, simmer about 2 hours until peas are tender and turn pasty. Cool and freeze in 6-cup container.

To serve, thaw soup and simmer until warmed through. If peas are too thick, add water to make consistency of thick soup.

SUMMARY OF PROCESSES:

Soak split peas in water overnight; cut ham in cubes; peel and slice $\frac{3}{4}$ cup carrots; chop 1 cup onion, $\frac{1}{3}$ cup celery.

FREEZE IN: 6-cup container
SERVE WITH: Orange and apple slices

Makes 6 servings

Italian Shepherd's Pie

1 pound bulk Italian sausage
½ cup chopped onions
3 large eggs beaten
1 14½-ounce can Italian-style stewed tomatoes
1 cup shredded Cheddar cheese
1 teaspoon dried basil
½ teaspoon fennel seeds
1 9-inch unbaked pastry shell

In large skillet cook sausage and onions until sausage is brown. Drain fat. Add and stir in beaten eggs, tomatoes, cheese, and spices. Spoon into pie shell. Wrap and freeze.

When thawed, place on a foil-lined baking sheet. Cover edge of pie with foil so that it does not brown too quickly. Bake at 375°F for 25 minutes. Remove foil; bake for 10 minutes more or until set.

For variety: Combine mashed potatoes, enough for 4 servings, and add ½ cup shredded cheddar cheese. Spoon over meat and sprinkle with paprika. Bake uncovered 20 minutes more. Let stand 5 to 10 minutes before serving.

SUMMARY OF PROCESSES:
Chop ½ cup onion.

FREEZE IN: 10-inch quiche or pie plate
SERVE WITH: Artichoke Hearts

Makes 4 to 5 servings

Bird's Nest Pie

1 16-ounce package spaghetti (use half)
2 large eggs, beaten
$\frac{1}{3}$ cup grated Parmesan cheese
$\frac{1}{2}$ cup finely chopped onion
2 tablespoons sweet butter
8 ounces sour cream
1 pound bulk Italian sausage
1 6-ounce can tomato paste
1 cup water
4 ounces sliced mozzarella cheese

Break spaghetti in half and cook as directed on package until al dente; drain. While spaghetti is warm, combine with eggs and Parmesan cheese. Press spaghetti into bottom and up sides of a well-greased, 10-inch pie plate with a spoon. Sauté onion in margarine for 5 minutes, mix with sour cream or yogurt, and spread over crust.

At the same time, cook sausage in a large skillet until brown, about 15 minutes. Drain the fat. Stir in tomato paste and water. Bring to a boil; reduce heat. Simmer uncovered 10 minutes, stirring occasionally. Spoon over sour cream mixture. Cover dish with foil and freeze. Put cheese slices in a 1-quart bag; attach to side of dish.

To prepare for serving, thaw pie and cheese. Bake pie uncovered in a preheated 350°F oven for 25 minutes. Arrange mozzarella slices on top; return pie to oven until cheese melts.

SUMMARY OF PROCESSES:

Chop $\frac{1}{2}$ cup onion; slice 4 ounces mozzarella cheese.

FREEZE IN: 10-inch quiche or pie plate; 1-quart freezer bag
SERVE WITH: Apple-Spinach Salad
NOTE: If you double this recipe, use 3 9-inch pie plates.

Makes 8 servings

Grilled Ham Slices

    2 pounds cooked ham
    1 cup regular, uncooked rice*

GLAZE
    $\frac{1}{4}$ cup brown sugar*
    1 tablespoon prepared mustard*
    2 teaspoons water
    1 tablespoon white vinegar or lemon juice*

Freeze ham slices in 1-gallon bag.

To serve, thaw ham slices. Prepare rice according to package directions. Mix remaining ingredients for glaze and spread over ham slices. Grill, broil, or barbeque ham slices 2 or 3 minutes per side, basting with sauce once per side.

SUMMARY OF PROCESSES:

Cut 2 pounds ham into $\frac{3}{8}$-inch-thick slices.

FREEZE IN: 1-gallon bag
SERVE WITH: Corn on the Cob with Chili Butter

Makes 4 servings

Glazed Ham

    3 pounds boneless ham
    3 tablespoons orange marmalade
    1 tablespoon Dijon mustard

Mix together the orange marmalade and Dijon mustard. Smear over the ham and freeze in 1-gallon freezer bag. When thawed, empty into Crock-Pot and cook on low for 6 to 8 hours.

    FREEZE IN: 1-gallon bag
    SERVE WITH: Spaghetti Squash; green beans

Makes 6 servings

Chili Dogs

    3 cups Grandma's Chili
    1 package beef franks*
    1 package hot dog buns
    1 cup grated Cheddar cheese

Store the beef franks, marked, in the refrigerator and freeze the cheese in a bag taped to the package of hot dog buns.
    When thawed warm the chili; cook the franks and serve on the buns sprinkled with Cheddar cheese.

    FREEZE IN: 3-cup container; 1-quart freezer bag
    SERVE WITH: Winter Fruit Salad

Makes 4 servings

Chicken Tetrazzini

1 16-ounce package spaghetti (use half)
$1\frac{1}{4}$ cups finely chopped onion
3 tablespoons sweet butter
1 cup chopped green bell pepper
$5\frac{1}{2}$ cups cooked, diced chicken
4 cups grated Monterey Jack cheese
2 $10\frac{3}{4}$-ounce cans cream of mushroom soup
$1\frac{1}{2}$ cups milk
Salt and pepper to taste

Break spaghetti in half and cook as directed on package until al dente; drain. Sauté onions in butter until transparent, about 10 minutes. Thoroughly mix onions and remaining ingredients with spaghetti in a large bowl. Put spaghetti mixture in 2 6-cup containers and freeze.

To prepare for serving, thaw Tetrazzini and put in a baking dish. Bake uncovered in a preheated 350°F oven until bubbly, about 30 to 40 minutes.

SUMMARY OF PROCESSES:

Dice $5\frac{1}{2}$ cups cooked chicken; chop 1 cup green bell pepper, $1\frac{1}{4}$ cups onion.

FREEZE IN: 2 6-cup containers
SERVE WITH: Gingered Carrots; chocolate cake

Makes 12 servings

Deborah's Sweet-and-Sour Chicken

$\frac{1}{2}$ cup sugar

3 tablespoons cornstarch

$\frac{1}{2}$ cup white vinegar

1 8-ounce can pineapple chunks (reserve juice)

$\frac{1}{4}$ cup soy sauce

$\frac{1}{2}$ teaspoon salt

$\frac{1}{2}$ teaspoon crushed garlic

$\frac{1}{2}$ teaspoon paprika

$\frac{1}{2}$ teaspoon ground ginger

1 cup coarsely chopped celery

1 cup coarsely chopped onion

3 cups cooked, diced chicken

1 cup coarsely chopped green bell pepper

1 4-ounce can mushroom stems and pieces, drained

1 8-ounce can sliced water chestnuts, drained

2 cups regular, uncooked rice*

In a medium saucepan, combine sugar and cornstarch; stir in white vinegar, juice from pineapple chunks, soy sauce, salt, garlic, paprika, ginger, celery, and onion. Bring to a boil; reduce heat. Simmer, stirring constantly until thickened, about 20 minutes. Remove from heat. Stir in pineapple chunks, chicken, bell pepper, mushrooms, and water chestnuts. Put in an 8-cup container and freeze.

To prepare for serving, thaw chicken and put in a baking dish treated with non-stick spray. Bake uncovered in a preheated 350°F oven for 45 minutes. Prepare rice according to package directions. Serve chicken over rice.

SUMMARY OF PROCESSES:

Coarsely chop 1 cup each: onion, celery, bell pepper; dice 3 cups cooked chicken.

FREEZE IN: 8-cup container

SERVE WITH: Sautéed Apples with Thyme; steamed broccoli tossed with toasted sesame seeds

Makes 8 servings

Chicken à la King

1 strip diced bacon
$\frac{1}{2}$ cup finely chopped onion
2 ounces mushroom stems and pieces (reserve $\frac{1}{4}$ cup liquid)
$\frac{1}{4}$ cup chopped green bell pepper
1 tablespoon sweet butter
$\frac{1}{4}$ cup all-purpose flour
1 teaspoon salt
$\frac{1}{4}$ teaspoon pepper
1 cup half-and-half
$\frac{2}{3}$ cup chicken broth
1 tablespoon sherry
1 cup cooked, diced chicken
1 tablespoon pimientos
1 package puff pastry shells*

In a large saucepan, cook and stir bacon, onion, mushrooms, and bell pepper in margarine over medium heat until vegetables are tender, about 10 minutes. Blend in flour, salt, and pepper. Cook over low heat, stirring constantly until well mixed.

Remove from heat. Stir in half-and-half, chicken broth, reserved mushroom liquid, and sherry. Heat to a boil, stirring constantly for 1 minute. Stir in chicken and pimientos. Allow chicken mixture to cool, put in a 1-gallon bag and freeze.

To prepare for serving, thaw puff pastry shells and chicken mixture. Heat in a large saucepan until bubbly, stirring constantly, about 15 minutes. Serve in warmed puff pastry shells.

SUMMARY OF PROCESSES:

Dice 1 strip bacon, 1 cup cooked chicken; chop $\frac{1}{2}$ cup onion, $\frac{1}{4}$ cup green bell pepper.

FREEZE IN: 1-gallon bag
SERVE WITH: Fresh-baked asparagus; red grapes or melon slices

Makes 4 to 5 servings

Southwestern Chicken Soup

    1 12-ounce jar salsa verde
    3 cups cooked, diced chicken
    1 15-ounce can cannellini beans, drained
    3 cups chicken broth
    1 teaspoon ground cumin
    2 green onions, chopped
    $\frac{1}{2}$ cup sour cream
    Tortilla chips (optional)

Empty the salsa into a large saucepan, cook 2 minutes over medium-high heat, then add the chicken, beans, broth, and cumin. Bring to a boil, lower heat to a simmer, and cook for 10 minutes, stirring occasionally.

When thawed, heat to boiling, then reduce heat and simmer 15 minutes. Top each bowl with sprinkling of onions, a dollop of sour cream, and some tortilla chips.

SUMMARY OF PROCESSES:

Dice 3 cups cooked chicken; chop 2 green onions.

FREEZE IN: 8-cup container
SERVE WITH: Watermelon Salad

Makes 4 servings

Lemon Chicken

1 teaspoon dried thyme leaves
1 teaspoon salt
$\frac{1}{2}$ teaspoon pepper
$\frac{1}{4}$ teaspoon crushed garlic
$\frac{1}{3}$ cup lemon juice
2 pounds boneless chicken pieces (breasts and/or thighs)
1 cup regular, uncooked rice*

Mix all the spices and lemon juice in a 1-gallon bag, add chicken pieces, and freeze.

When thawed, preheat oven to 450°F. Arrange chicken skin side down in a 8×8×2-inch baking dish treated with nonstick spray. Pour liquid over chicken. Bake 20 minutes. Turn chicken over and baste it. Bake 15 to 20 minutes longer or until chicken is tender and no longer pink when cut along the bone. Prepare rice according to package directions. Serve chicken over rice.

FREEZE IN: 1-gallon bag
SERVE WITH: Cucumber Salad; Roasted Grape Tomatoes

Makes 4 servings

Chicken and Rice Pilaf

    4 boneless, skinless chicken breasts
Salt, pepper, paprika to taste
1$\frac{1}{4}$ cups chicken broth
    1 cup regular uncooked rice
    1 envelope dry onion soup
    1 10$\frac{3}{4}$-ounce can condensed cream of mushroom soup
    2 tablespoons pimientos

Sprinkle chicken breasts with salt, pepper, and paprika. Mix chicken broth, uncooked rice, onion soup mix, cream of mushroom soup, and pimientos together; put in an 11×7×1$\frac{1}{2}$-inch baking dish. Place chicken breasts on top of rice mixture. Cover dish with foil and freeze.

To prepare for serving, thaw chicken dish. Bake uncovered in a preheated 375°F oven 1$\frac{1}{4}$ hours or until chicken and rice are tender.

FREEZE IN: 11×7×1$\frac{1}{2}$-inch baking dish
SERVE WITH: Tomato Caprese; baked asparagus

Makes 4 servings

Oriental Chicken

2 tablespoons sweet butter
2 tablespoons all-purpose flour
1 cup chicken broth
1 cup water
1 tablespoon soy sauce
1 teaspoon crushed garlic
1 cups cooked, diced chicken
$\frac{1}{8}$ teaspoon pepper
1 5-ounce can chow mein noodles*

Melt butter in a medium saucepan over low heat. Add flour and stir over medium heat until bubbly. Add broth, water, soy sauce, garlic powder, chicken, and pepper; simmer for 5 minutes. Cool and freeze in a 1-gallon bag.

To prepare for serving, thaw chicken mixture and heat in a pan until bubbly. Serve over chow mein noodles.

SUMMARY OF PROCESSES:

Dice 2 cups cooked chicken.

FREEZE IN: 1-gallon bag
SERVE WITH: Sautéed Napa Cabbage; egg rolls; fortune cookies

Makes 4 servings

7

Table-Talk Questions

Dinner table conversation builds a sense of security and family identity in children, and helps us understand one another better as we tune into each other's day. In addition, studies of students who excel in school point to the benefit of directed conversation at a family dinner table, where each family member has his or her say, and then waits to hear the views of others.

Try some of these topics with your family, and with company, too.

1. Talk about one thing you started today and one thing you finished.
2. Is faster always better? Talk about when it is and when it isn't.
3. What worries you most?
4. Devise a family plan for evacuation of your home in case of fire.
5. Of what are you proudest?
6. If you could do anything you want as a career, what would it be?
7. Give a sincere compliment to the person on your right.
8. Which of your friends' parents do you respect most and why?

9. What does it mean to be patriotic?
10. What would you most like to change about yourself?
11. Read a list of state capitals. Going around the table, each person must try to match the state with the capital.
12. Start a story. After a few sentences, the next person must to add to it and so on around the table.
13. (With young children) Tell us about a picture you drew today.
14. Discuss upcoming events or lifestyle changes that will affect your family, for example a new job, a new teacher or level in school, or the failing health of a grandparent.
15. What is one new thing you'd like to try?
16. Where is one place you would like to visit?
17. How can you help people in your workplace?
18. What is your favorite smell or fragrance?
19. If you ran for a political office, what would it be? What would be your central campaign issue?
20. Tell about a time you broke a bone or were injured in some way.
21. What is your favorite song?
22. Mom and Dad tell what they worried about most and what they liked most when they were children.
23. Ask grandparents to reminisce about colorful characters in their families.
24. What are some of your family traditions?
25. Play family trivia: Where did Dad and Mom meet? How many second cousins do you have? What was the name of your first pet?
26. Talk about salaries. Give five or six examples of average earnings for various occupations. *Do* wages necessarily match the value or significance of the work done?
27. Share a memory that goes way, way back in your childhood.
28. What is the best thing that happened to you today? The worst thing?
29. What is the funniest thing that happened to you today?
30. Bring a newspaper clipping and discuss a character quality it exemplified, such as greed, courage, disregard for human life.
31. Tell a favorite memory from a wedding you attended.
32. Read excerpts from a letter recently written to the family.
33. What was the most interesting thing you learned today?
34. Tell about the main character in a book you're reading and the challenge he or she is facing.
35. What is the saddest movie or television show that you have watched?
36. If you could be a guest in anyone's home, whom would you choose?

37. Why do you like some people and dislike some others?
38. What would be your ideal vacation?
39. What is your favorite Christmas decoration? How did it become special to you?
40. Find and read a poem expressive of the current season.
41. Tell what someone said today that made you feel good about yourself.
42. If you could change one physical feature, what would it be?
43. What characteristics do you see in you that came from your father or mother?
44. What qualities would you like to emulate from your parent or relatives?
45. Who is your favorite relative?
46. If you won the lottery, how would it change your life?
47. Tell about a time you were frightened.
48. Discuss how to shut off the water to the house.
49. Which holiday has the most meaning for you and why?
50. How do different types of music affect you?
51. What was your favorite childhood storybook? Why did you like it?
52. What is your favorite time of the day? Your favorite season?
53. Where do you want to be in ten years?
54. Tell about a figure in literature (or on television) who has impacted your life.
55. If you could live in a different century, what century would it be?
56. For what purpose were you born?
57. Describe what you like best or least about the current season.
58. If you could change your first name, what name would you chose and why?
59. If you could be a professional in sports, what sport would you chose?
60. Plan a favorite dinner party. What food would you serve? Who would you invite? Where would you have the party?
61. If you could own a store, what kind would it be?
62. If you had one chance to grab something of value as your house burned, what would it be?
63. (With children) Have one family member cover both eyes. Let the rest of the family help that person eat. Talk about what it would be like to be blind.
64. (With children) Put a cotton ball in each ear. Then cover the ears with a wool hat. Discuss what it would be like to be hearing-impaired.
65. (With children) What is the hardest part of a teacher's job?
66. (With children) If you could be like any older person, who would you be like?
67. (With children) What would you do with your time if you didn't have a television?
68. (With children) What would you like to ask the president (or a historical figure)?

69. What would you like to ask your great-grandparents?
70. What do you like best or worst about being your age?
71. (With children) If you could fly, where would you go?
72. What is one of the best gifts you have ever given?
73. What is a favorite memory you have with your parent or sibling?
74. If you could give $1,000 away, to whom would you give it and why?
75. What is the nicest thing you've done recently for an elderly or disabled person?
76. (With children) "Sticks and stones can break my bones . . ." What words have hurt you?
77. If you were caught in a snowstorm, in the car, with a winter coat, what would you do to survive?
78. If you could buy any car, what would it be?
79. "Over the river and through the woods to Grandmother's house we go." What landmarks do you remember passing on the way to your grandmother's house?
80. What are some objects that you particularly remember from a grandparent's house?
81. Where is the most beautiful place you've ever been?
82. What was your favorite comic book superhero?
83. Tell about a favorite memory of a grandparent.
84. Tell about a prize or an award you won.
85. If you were to live in another country for a year, what would you miss the most?
86. What foods do you most dislike?
87. Tell about a time when you were homesick.
88. Tell about a favorite teacher.

8

Accompaniments

Many of the following recipes are provided by Rebecca Pasquariello of Savor Fresh Foods. Rebecca's passion is to bring people back to the table. "Dining is a time to savor family and friends; it is not just a time to eat," she says. "Offering our clients the opportunity to slow down from their hectic lifestyles and enjoy the pleasures of the table once again is one of our proudest accomplishments."

Choose seasonal fruits and vegetables, they are the least expensive at their peak of taste, color, and nutrition. Try adding one new fresh vegetable a week to your family meals.

Spring Vegetables

Sautéed Spinach

   2 cups spinach, shredded
   2 cloves garlic, crushed
   4 teaspoons olive oil
   salt and pepper

Heat olive oil and garlic in a pan. Stir in spinach and wilt it down. Add salt and pepper. You can substitute 2 cups collard greens or arugula for the spinach.

Crudités

   snap peas
   jicama sticks
   carrot
   celery sticks
   red pepper strips

Dip crudités in hummus or ranch dip. Fun for the whole family and a quick side for pizza night.

Asparagus Italiano

   1 pound trimmed asparagus stalks
   $\frac{1}{4}$ pound thin-sliced ham, pepperoni, or prosciutto
   salt and pepper

Wrap big pepperoni slices, thin ham slices, or prosciutto around asparagus stalks and place seam side down in baking dish. Salt and pepper. Bake at 400°F for 10 to 15 minutes.

Mango and Avocado

1 mango, peeled and sliced
1 avocado, peeled and sliced
2 teaspoons lemon juice
salt and pepper

Arrange mango and avocado slices on a plate. Sprinkle with lemon juice, salt and pepper.

Artichoke Hearts

1 artichokes (or $\frac{1}{2}$ artichoke per person)
$\frac{1}{2}$ lemon, for squeezing

Cut $\frac{1}{3}$ off the top of fresh artichoke, trim remaining leaves, cut stem off so that it will sit flat in a microwave-safe dish. Place artichokes in dish, squeeze lemon juice over, add 3 tablespoons water, and cover with plastic wrap. Microwave on high for 12 to 15 minutes. Serve with herby butter.

Apple-Spinach Salad

2 cups baby spinach
2 cups romaine lettuce
1 Granny Smith apple, sliced
$\frac{1}{4}$ cup cashew nuts (toasted, optional)

DRESSING:

1 cup olive oil
$\frac{1}{3}$ cup vinegar
kosher salt
fresh ground pepper
celery salt
garlic salt

Toss spinach, letture, apple slices, and cashews. Add desired amount of dressing. Refrigerate remaining dressing for another salad.

Makes 4 servings

Spicy Grilled Pineapple

1 pineapple
2–3 teaspoons olive oil
$\frac{1}{2}$ teaspoon cayenne
salt

Slice peel off pineapple and cut it horizontally into rounds. Toss with olive oil, a little cayenne, and salt. Place on grill and cook until charred and tender, turning once, 8 to 12 minutes. Great with tuna or pork.

Gingered Carrots

18 mini carrots
 4 cups canned chicken broth or water
 2 tablespoons sweet butter
 2 tablespoons brown sugar
 2 tablespoons finely minced crystallized ginger
 2 teaspoons ground ginger

Place carrots in saucepan with broth and bring to boil. Reduce heat and cook 15 minutes or until tender. Drain and return carrots to pot. Melt butter in small saucepan and add other ingredients. Pour butter mixture over carrots and warm about 2 minutes on low heat. Salt and pepper to taste.

Summer Vegetables

Oven-Roasted Broccoli

2 cups broccoli florets
4 large cloves garlic, peeled and smashed
2 tablespoons olive oil
salt and pepper

Toss broccoli with olive oil, garlic, salt, and pepper. Roast at 400°F for 20 minutes.

Broiled Tomatoes

4 medium tomatoes
3 tablespoons olive oil
salt
$\frac{1}{2}$ cup bread crumbs, Parmesan, or a mix of both

Slice tomatoes in half. Sprinkle with olive oil, salt, and bread crumbs or Parmesan cheese. Broil about 6 minutes.

Roasted Grape Tomatoes

3 pint grape tomatoes (15 to 20)
2 tablespoons peeled and smashed garlic
2 tablespoons olive oil
salt and pepper

Toss grape tomatoes with olive oil, salt, pepper, and garlic and roast them at 400°F for 10 minutes.

Sautéed Napa Cabbage

  1 head napa cabbage, rough chop
  2 tablespoons olive oil
  1 garlic clove, minced
  1 tablespoon fresh ginger, minced
  $\frac{1}{2}$ cup rice wine vinegar

Roughly chop cabbage. To hot pan add oil, garlic, ginger, and cabbage and toss until slightly wilted. Leave crunchy. Add $\frac{1}{2}$ cup rice wine vinegar at the end. Salt and pepper to taste.

Cauliflower Mock Potato Salad

Use your favorite potato salad recipe, except that you will use cauliflower in place of the potatoes (no peeling!). Boil cauliflower until pretty soft (texture of a cooked potato). Cut it up a little smaller than you would a potato (nickel size). Add ingredients for potato salad.

Watermelon Salad

1 (5-pound) watermelon seedless
1 Vidalia or red sweet onion, thinly sliced
$\frac{1}{4}$ cup red wine vinegar
salt and pepper
$\frac{1}{2}$ cup extra-virgin olive oil
2 tablespoons chopped fresh mint
4 ounces feta cheese, crumbled
6 whole mint sprigs

Peel and cut the flesh from the melon into bite-size pieces, removing and discarding the seeds, and set aside. Peel and slice the onion into rings.

In a small bowl, combine the vinegar, salt, and pepper, and whisk until salt is dissolved. Slowly whisk in the olive oil. Add in the chopped mint, taste, and adjust seasonings. In a large bowl, combine the melon, onion, and feta. Pour the dressing over the melon mixture and toss gently until everything is coated and evenly mixed. Garnish with mint sprigs.

Roasted Corn on the Cob with Chili Butter

6 ears of corn
6 tablespoons sweet butter ($\frac{3}{4}$ stick)
salt and pepper
6 ice cubes

CHILI BUTTER

1 stick sweet butter
1 tablespoon chili powder
Salt and pepper

Shuck the corn. Place each ear of corn on a piece of foil. Add 1 teaspoon butter, salt and pepper to taste, and 1 ice cube to each piece of foil. Wrap them up and place on grill. Grill for 25 minutes, turning once. Serve with the chili butter.

Chili Butter: Roll the grilled corn in 1 cup melted butter that has been seasoned with salt, pepper, and chili powder.

Greek Pasta Salad

    penne pasta (16-ounce box)
1 red pepper, julliened
1 Bermuda onion, cut in half and sliced
1 cup black or kalamata olives
4 tomatoes, chopped
1 cucumber, sliced
3 tablespoons fresh basil leaves (chiffonade)
    Salt and pepper to taste

DRESSING

$\frac{1}{3}$ cup red wine vinegar
$\frac{2}{3}$ cup olive oil

    Boil pasta and drain. Mix dressing in small bowl. In large bowl toss together pasta and vegetables. Add desired amount of dressing and toss to coat.

Makes 8 servings

Tomatoes Caprese

6 ripe tomatoes, sliced
4 balls of fresh mozzarella cheese, sliced
    olive oil
    salt and pepper
    fresh basil
    balsamic vinegar

    Arrange tomato slices and mozzarella on plate. Drizzle with olive oil, salt and pepper, fresh basil, and balsamic vinegar if desired.

Cucumber Salad

2 large cucumbers
1 medium red or yellow onion
3 tablespoons olive oil
4 teaspoons apple cider vinegar
salt and pepper

Slice cucumbers. Salt them and set in a strainer for 30 minutes. Rinse cucumbers and squeeze out the liquid with paper towels. Add sliced onion. Toss with olive oil, apple cider vinegar, salt, and pepper. Cover and chill until ready to serve and flavors have come together.

Autumn and Winter Vegetables

Spaghetti Squash

1 spaghetti squash
3 tablespoons olive oil
3 garlic cloves, peeled and smashed
salt and pepper
fresh basil
fresh parsley
grated Parmesan cheese

Prick squash in several places. Cook in microwave 20 minutes (check and rotate at 10 minutes until squash gives slightly when pressed. Remove from microwave oven and let stand 5 minutes or until cool enough to handle. Cut squash in half lengthwise. Remove seeds. Shred squash with a fork and set aside. Heat a nonstick pan over medium-high heat, add olive oil, toss with salt and pepper, garlic, basil, parsley, and Parmesan cheese for a delicious side. Or toss with your favorite jarred spaghetti sauce for a new take on a family favorite.

Roasted Cauliflower

1 head cauliflower
$\frac{1}{3}$ cup chicken broth
$\frac{1}{3}$ cup olive oil
$\frac{1}{3}$ cup white wine or water
3 cloves thinly sliced garlic
1 tablespoon Italian parsley, chopped
2 teaspoons dried oregano
salt and pepper to taste
3 tablespoons butter
$\frac{1}{2}$ cup dried bread crumbs
2 tablespoons olive oil
2 tablespoons Parmesan cheese

Preheat the oven to 400°F.

Cut cauliflower into chunks (discarding hard center stem) and place in baking dish.

Drizzle with equal amounts of chicken broth, olive oil, and white wine, about $\frac{1}{3}$ cup each. Add thinly sliced garlic, a pinch of oregano, chopped Italian parsley, and salt and pepper to taste. Dab the top with a bit of butter. Cover the pan with aluminum foil and bake until tender, about 30 minutes. The florets should fall apart if you poke them with your finger. Remove foil and top with bread crumbs that have been tossed with a little olive oil and Parmesan. Let brown another 15 minutes.

Parsnip Fries

4 parsnips, peeled, quartered, and cut into sticks
2 tablespoons olive oil
salt and pepper to taste

Preheat oven to 475°F.

Peel parsnips. Quarter lengthwise and cut into little sticks. Place on large rimmed baking sheet and toss with olive oil, salt and pepper. Roast 15 to 20 minutes and toss. Continue roasting for 10 to 15 minutes.

Sautéed Apples with Thyme

3 apples
2 tablespoons sweet butter
1 teaspoon fresh chopped thyme (or $\frac{1}{4}$ teaspoon dried)
2 teaspoons grated lemon zest
salt and pepper

Core and cut each apple into 8 wedges.

Heat butter in skillet over medium heat. Add apples, fresh thyme, and grated lemon zest. Season with salt and pepper and sauté until apples are just tender when pierced with knife.

Twice-Baked Sweet Potatoes

4 sweet potatoes, scrubbed and dried
2–4 tablespoons butter
1 small can crushed pineapple
1 teaspoon each allspice, cinnamon, and nutmeg
salt and pepper to taste

Preheat oven 400°F.

Place potatoes directly on rack in center of oven and bake 30 minutes.

Pierce each potato with a fork and continue cooking until tender, about 30 to 40 minutes more.

Remove from oven. Cut potatoes in half, scoop out flesh to create canoelike shape.

Mash potatoes slightly with fork, add butter, pineapple, and spices. Salt and pepper to taste.

Refill the potato shells with mixture, mounding slightly.

Red Peppers and Pears with Cilantro Dressing.

2 red bell peppers, stemmed and seeded
3 fresh pears, stemmed and cored

CILANTRO DRESSING

$\frac{1}{4}$ cup fresh lime juice
$\frac{1}{4}$ cup olive oil
3 tablespoons chopped cilantro
1 fresh jalapeño, chopped (*decrease or omit the seeds and membranes if you don't want it very hot and spicy)
1 clove garlic, minced
$\frac{1}{2}$ teaspoon chili powder
$\frac{1}{2}$ teaspoon ground cumin

Slice fresh red peppers and pears. Toss with Cilantro Dressing.

Anytime Vegetables and Fruit

Steamed Edamame

1 1-pound bag frozen edamame
kosher or sea salt to taste

Steam or blanche edamame. Drain and toss with kosher or sea salt. Squeeze bean into mouth and pull skin out with teeth. Fun! Fun! Fun! (Edamame can be found in the freezer section of many supermarkets.)

Asian Slaw

1 cup red and green cabbage
2 large carrots
$\frac{1}{4}$ cup cilantro
1 large red bell pepper
1 cup edamame
salt

Shred 1 cup red cabbaage and green cabbage. Grate 2 carrots. Chop one large red bell pepper. Chop $\frac{1}{4}$ cup cilantro. Pop the skins off 1 cup thawed, blanched edamame. Toss and sprinkle with salt to taste.

Italian Parsley Salad

1 cup Italian parsley (flat-leaf parsley), leaves pulled and stems removed
$\frac{1}{2}$ cup grated carrots
salt and pepper to taste
2 tablespoons olive oil
$\frac{1}{4}$ cup fresh lemon juice

A new twist on a fresh salad. Toss all ingredients together and serve.

Classic Roasted New Potatoes

2 pounds red new potatoes
$\frac{1}{4}$ cup olive oil
4 whole garlic cloves, peeled
salt and pepper to taste
Thai fish sauce

Preheat oven to 425°F. Quarter potatoes and place on rimmed baking sheet. Add whole garlic cloves and drizzle with olive oil, salt, and pepper, and toss to coat. Roast for 25 minutes. Turn potatoes with spatula and continue roasting for 20 to 25 minutes more or until golden and tender.

When potatoes are finished, toss with desired herbs—fresh or dried, whatever you have on hand—such as Italian parsley, basil, thyme, or rosemary. The secret is adding 1 to 2 teaspoons Thai fish sauce, which can be found in your regular grocery store in the Asian aisle.

Makes 4 servings

Dressings

Vinaigrette

$\frac{1}{4}$ teaspoon Dijon mustard
1 teaspoon kosher salt
$\frac{1}{8}$ teaspoon black pepper
3 tablespoon vinegar (of choice, or lemon juice, or any citrus juice)
1 cup oil (or half olive and half canola)
optional ingredients: shallots, flavored vinegars, herbs, or citrus

Shake these ingredients together in a jar. Put in blender with blueberries or strawberries or raspberries that are about to go yucky. Use a berry vinaigrette for spinach salad. For sherry vinaigrette: substitute $\frac{1}{3}$ cup sherry instead of the 3 tablespoons vinegar. Add shallots.

Makes $1\frac{1}{4}$ cups

Creamy Dressing

$\frac{1}{4}$ cup mayonnaise
1 garlic clove, minced
1 tablespoon whole-grain mustard
juice of 1 lemon
salt and pepper

Mix in blender or food processor.

Caesar Dressing with Thai Fish Sauce

4 heaping tablespoons quality mayonnaise
1 clove garlic, crushed
juice and zest of 1 lemon
2 tablespoons Thai fish sauce
$\frac{1}{2}$ cup grated Parmesan cheese
2 teaspoons Worcestershire sauce
1 teaspoon coarse black pepper
3 tablespoons extra-virgin olive oil

Whisk by hand or blend in the food processor until emulsified

Salads Miscellaneous Ideas

Hearts of Palm Salad

1 can hearts of palm, drained and sliced
1 large tomato, diced
1 large cucumber, diced
1 can marinated artichoke hearts, drained
$\frac{1}{2}$ red onion, sliced

Combine hearts of palm, tomato, cucumber, artichoke, and red onion; toss with a simple vinaigrette.

Lentil Salad

$\frac{1}{4}$ cup red wine vinegar
3 tablespoons olive oil
$1\frac{1}{4}$ cup lentils
1 large cucumber, diced
$\frac{1}{2}$ cup finely chopped Italian parsley (flat-leaf parsley)
$\frac{1}{2}$ cup finely chopped red onion
salt and pepper

Cook lentils according to directions (or use canned lentils, rinsed). Whip together vinegar and oil. Add lentils, cucumber, parsley, red onion, salt and pepper. Toss. Lentils are always in. Try this recipe chilled like a salad or mixed with roasted veggies and feta cheese for a warm side.

Winter Fruit Salad

1 red grapefruit, peeled, seeded, and separated
1 orange, peeled, seeded, and separated
1 kiwi, peeled and sliced
2 avocados, peeled and sliced
lettuce
Sweet Vidalia Onion Salad Dressing

Toss fruit in the dressing and arrange on lettuce.

Cookies

I could hear the children coming home from school. One of them shouted to the others, "Cookies at our house! I can smell them from here!" Soon the kitchen was full of expectant faces. The smell of cookies baking had worked its charm again. Like invisible fingers, it had drawn people into the home.

I had arrived only a few minutes before the school bus, but planning ahead with frozen dough ensured the warm, yummy welcome. I had four different bags of frozen, formed cookie dough from the following recipes.

Ginger Cookies

$1\frac{1}{2}$ cup shortening

2 cup sugar

2 large eggs

2 teaspoon vanilla extract

$\frac{1}{2}$ cup molasses

4 cups flour

4 teaspoons baking soda

2 teaspoons ground cinnamon

2 teaspoons ground nutmeg

2 teaspoons ground cloves

2 teaspoons ground ginger

2 teaspoons salt

Cream together shortening and sugar. Add eggs, vanilla, and molasses. Mix well. Add remaining ingredients. Roll into 1-inch balls and dip in sugar. Place on cookie sheet that has been lined with waxed paper. Freeze all balls of dough. Then place in batches of 12 balls of dough into small Ziploc bags and seal. Label bag with recipe name and baking instructions.

To serve, preheat oven to 375°F. Place 12 balls of frozen dough on prepared cookie sheet and bake for 10 minutes or until lightly brown. Cool slightly before removing from pan.

Barb's White Chocolate Chip Macadamia Nut Cookies

$\frac{1}{2}$ cup unsalted butter

$\frac{1}{2}$ cup shortening

$\frac{3}{4}$ cup sugar

$\frac{1}{2}$ cup brown sugar

1 egg

$1\frac{1}{2}$ cup flour

1 teaspoon baking soda

$\frac{1}{2}$ tsp salt

2 teaspoons vanilla extract

12 ounces white chocolate chips

$\frac{1}{2}$ cup chopped macadamia nuts (toasted per instructions below)

First, lightly toast macadamia nuts in the oven for approximately 5 minutes at 275°F. This makes a great difference. Set nuts aside.

Cream butter and shortening. Gradually add sugar and beat until light and fluffy. Add eggs and mix well. Combine flour, soda, and salt and add to creamed mixture. Blend in vanilla and stir in white chocolate chips and nuts.

Line baking sheet with waxed paper and drop heaping teaspoons of dough over the whole cookie sheet. Freeze the balls. When frozen, put 12 cookie dough balls each in small Ziploc bags. Label bag with recipe name and baking instructions. Freeze.

To serve, preheat oven to 350°F and place 12 balls of dough about 3 inches apart on a prepared cookie sheet. Bake 13 minutes. Cool slightly before removing from pan.

Erica's Oatmeal Cookies with White Chocolate

1 cup unsalted butter
1 cup brown sugar
$\frac{1}{2}$ cup granulated sugar
2 large eggs
1 teaspoon vanilla extract
$\frac{1}{2}$ cup flour
1 teaspoon baking soda
$\frac{1}{2}$ teaspoon salt
3 cup oats (quick or old-fashioned)
1 12-ounce package white chocolate chips

Beat together butter and sugars until creamy. Add eggs and vanilla; beat well. Add combined flour, baking soda, oats, and salt; mix well. Stir in white chocolate chips. Drop by rounded tablespoons onto cookie sheet that has been lined with waxed paper. Freeze. When frozen, place 12 cookies dough balls each into small Ziploc bags. Label bag with recipe name and baking instructions. Freeze.

To serve, preheat oven to 350°F. Place 12 balls of dough on prepared cookie sheet. Bake 10 to 12 minutes until golden brown. Cool 1 minute on cookie sheet; remove to wire rack.

Reese's Chewy Chocolate Cookies

    2 cups flour
    $\frac{3}{4}$ cup cocoa
    1 teaspoon baking soda
    $\frac{1}{2}$ teaspoon salt
    $1\frac{1}{4}$ cup butter
    2 cups sugar
    2 large eggs
    2 teaspoons vanilla extract
    1 8-ounce package Reese's Peanut Butter Chips

Stir together dry ingredients. Beat butter and sugar in a large bowl with mixer until fluffy. Add eggs and vanilla; beat well. Gradually add flour mixture, beat well. Stir in peanut chips. Drop by rounded teaspoon onto cookie sheet that has been lined with waxed paper. Freeze dough. When frozen take 12 dough balls each and seal in small Ziploc bags. Label bag with recipe name and baking instructions. Freeze.

To serve, preheat oven to 350°F and place 12 balls of dough on prepared cookie sheet. Bake 11 to 13 minutes or until edges are lightly brown. (Do not over-bake; cookies will be soft. They will puff up while baking and flatten while cooling.) Cool slightly and remove from cookie sheet to wire rack. Cool completely.

Tips

TABASCO

If something is flat-tasting, add two shakes of Tabasco—not for the heat, but because it brings up the flavor.

BLANCHING

Blanching vegetables helps set the vivid color and the texture. Submerge cut vegetables in boiling water for 30 seconds to 1 minute. Then submerge immediately after in ice water. If desired, then quickly sauté the vegetables in butter, or oil to bring them back up to heat.

GRILLING VEGETABLES

You can grill almost any vegetable. Choose three vegetables in equal proportions from the following list: onion, asparagus, mushrooms, zucchini, squash, corn, eggplant, tomatoes, sweet potatoes. Slice veggies. Put in big bowl. Sprinkle generously with olive oil, kosher salt, fresh ground pepper, and whole garlic cloves. Mix well and set aside, covered. Put on a layer of aluminum foil on hot a grill and cook 10 to 20 minutes.

OLIVE OIL

The first press of the olives is extra-virgin. Second or third press is virgin. Everything left over is olive oil. It's 80% olive oil and 20% canola or other oil. But use pure olive oil if possible.

Use extra-virgin oil on top of salad but do not cook with it. Heating will make extra-virgin oil taste bitter.

9

Adapting the Once-a-Month Method

Choosing recipes

Once you've tried *Once-a-Month Cooking,* you may want to adapt it to your own recipes. The following suggestions will help you set up your system:

Choose dishes that freeze well. (See the section on freezer storage tips in chapter 10.) Take into consideration that it's not safe to thaw meat, work with it, leave it raw, and then refreeze it. You must cook meat before freezing it again. But if you buy fresh meat, you can add ingredients and freeze the meat raw.

Start with your family's favorite recipes rather than exotic, new dishes. Or test recipes before you create your own plan. Be sure to pick simple recipes rather than ones that require many complicated steps. You need to keep your assembly order and food preparation as simple as possible. Otherwise, you'll be defeating your purpose of saving time.

Make sure you have a nice variety of recipes. You don't want to serve similar entrées too close together, such as two stews or three creamy noodle casseroles. If you don't mind eating the same dish twice in a month, double the recipe for a favorite entrée, divide it in half, and freeze it. You may also want to consider dishes that could be used for both lunch and dinner, or that could be taken to work and reheated in a microwave.

If you enjoy cooking for others, choose some dishes that work well for company or could be taken to someone who is sick or has a special need.

After you decide what recipes you want to try, divide them into groups such as chicken, beef, fish, pork, meatless, or miscellaneous. This will show you how many recipes you have in each category. You may have too many chicken dishes or casseroles and need to balance your recipes by adding other kinds of meats or different types of dishes.

You may want to set up your system for only a week's worth of dishes rather than two weeks or a month. Or you may want to spread out the process, preparing all the dishes in a category at the same time—all the beef recipes in one afternoon, for example, and all the recipes in another category the next day.

Finally, make sure the ingredients called for in the recipes fit your budget. Some meats, especially fish, can be expensive.

Making a Menu Calendar

First, reproduce and use a blank calendar page. Record names of recipes on it in pencil, so if you need to you can move them around.

Next, check your schedule for days the family will be away from home and won't need meals; cross off those dates. Take into account the nights you'll need to prepare something quick because you or your kids have meetings or activities. Pencil in easy-to-prepare dishes for those times. Make note of holidays or special occasions, such as a birthday or anniversary, which will require special planning.

Organize your recipes by category, such as beef, chicken, or miscellaneous, before filling out the menu calendar. Make sure you will serve a variety of entrées for each week.

If you plan to have company, select the recipes you would use for the occasion, and write these entrées on the appropriate dates. Do the same with dishes you want to take to a friend or to a potluck dinner. For dates when the adults will be away but the kids will be eating at home, choose dishes the children like and that they or a baby-sitter can easily finish preparing.

If some dishes suit a particular day of the week, such as quiche on Sunday, add those recipes to the appropriate days. Then complete the calendar with your recipes.

Perhaps you want to create your own plan without considering your schedule or special occasions? You just want to prepare two weeks or a month of meals at once and have them in your freezer. If you do that, you may still want to fill out a calendar so you have a variety of meals scheduled. It's also a way to keep track of the ones you've made. Check them off as you serve them to your family.

Figuring Shopping and Staples Lists

Use your recipes to compile your shopping and staples lists. You'll need a page for each list. It may help to categorize your grocery list with the same headings we've used in this book: Canned Goods; Grains, Pasta, and Rice; Dry Ingredients and Seasonings; Frozen Foods; Dairy Products; Meat and Poultry; and Produce. (You can also categorize your list by aisles or areas in your favorite supermarket.)

To figure what food you'll need, check ingredients in each recipe, and record all the items on either the grocery shopping or staples lists. For example, if a recipe calls for cinnamon and you already have it, put it on the staples list. But add it to the shopping list if you don't have it. If six pounds of boneless chicken are required, put them on the shopping list. For items needed for more than one recipe, such as onions, ground beef, or tomato sauce, keep a running tally of quantities needed, and then figure the total. (See Equivalent Measure in chapter 10 for how to convert the size of portions.)

Finally, be sure to list freezer bags or containers you will need in order to freeze each entrée. Then add them to your shopping list.

Setting Up and Assembly Order

Once you've filled in your calendar, check instructions in The Day Before Cooking Day and Cooking Day Assembly Order sections for the two-week and one-month plans to help you make out your own assembly order.

Spread your recipes out on a table, arranging them in an order that will flow well when you're preparing them. Group recipes together that use similar ingredients, particularly meats.

Once you have your recipes in order, go through each one, tallying the total amount of each food item you'll need to process: how many onions to chop, carrots to shred, or pounds of ground beef to brown.

When you write out the assembly order, try to work with two or three recipes in the same category at a time, such as all the ground beef recipes or all the chicken. Record all the ingredients you'll need to store or freeze until the accompanying dishes are served. List all tasks you'll need to do the day before cooking day, such as cooking all the chicken or soaking pinto beans. You may also want to plan to do most of the chopping, grating, shredding, and slicing tasks the day before or first thing on cooking day. Recipes that require longer cooking, such as soups or stews, should also be started early in the day.

Make sure you'll have enough burners to cook dishes in a particular group at the same time. Whenever possible, combine steps for several dishes: cook rice for two dishes; sauté all onions at once.

Continue through all the recipes until you have completed your assembly order. Allow for time between groups of recipes so you can take some breaks.

Evaluating Your Plan

The first time you try your own plan, take a few extra minutes to write out any corrections in the recipes or procedures. That way, the next time you cook it will go even more smoothly.

THE FOLLOWING SUGGESTIONS WILL HELP YOU
REVISE YOUR PLAN:

Correct the order of tasks if they weren't easy to follow or in the right order. If you would do any part of the procedure differently, write on a notes sheet what you would do. If you should have prepared some dishes sooner rather than later in the process, make note of it.

Rework your plan if you had too many or too few dishes to prepare at once. Write out new directions, if the originals were difficult to follow in any of the sections. If necessary, correct "Ingredients Needed" on your shopping list.

10

Equipment: Special Help

EQUIVALENT MEASURES

      1 tablespoon = 3 teaspoons, $\frac{1}{2}$ fluid ounce

      2 tablespoons = 1 fluid ounce

      4 tablespoons = $\frac{1}{4}$ cup

      $5\frac{1}{3}$ tablespoons = $\frac{1}{3}$ cup

      8 tablespoons = $\frac{1}{2}$ cup

      12 tablespoons = $\frac{3}{4}$ cup

      16 tablespoons = 1 cup

      1 cup = $\frac{1}{2}$ pint or 8 fluid ounces

      2 cups = 1 pint

      2 pints = 1 quart

      16 cups = 4 quarts or 1 liquid gallon

      1 pound lean ground beef or sausage browned and drained = $2\frac{1}{2}$ cups

      1 pound cubed ham = 3 cups

      1 cooked, deboned whole chicken (about 4 pounds) diced = $4\frac{1}{2}$ cups

1 pound boneless, skinless chicken cooked and diced $= 2\frac{3}{4}$ cups
1 medium yellow onion, chopped $= 1\frac{1}{4}$ cups
1 medium yellow onion, chopped and sautéed $= \frac{3}{4}$ cup
1 medium green pepper, chopped $= 1$ cup
1 pound cheese, grated $= 4$ cups
3 ounces fresh mushrooms, sliced $= 1$ cup
1 pound zucchini, diced $= 1\frac{1}{2}$ cups
1 medium clove garlic, minced $= 1$ teaspoon

More Freezer Storage Tips

Frozen foods keep their natural color, flavor, and nutritive qualities better than canned or dried foods. Freezing also stops the bacterial action in fresh food that causes it to spoil.

Food kept in the freezer too long may not taste right, but it shouldn't make you sick. However, it's not safe to thaw food, especially meat, and then refreeze it without first cooking it.

Freezing food in moisture-proof containers with airtight lids or seals will help it keep its color and flavor much longer. You'll get the best results with products made for freezer use: plastic containers with lids, heavy aluminum foil, heavy plastic bags, freezer wraps, and tape. Glass jars with lids (leave head space for the food to expand when it freezes) also work well.

Avoid using regular wax paper; lightweight aluminum foil; regular plastic wrap; cartons from cottage cheese, ice cream, or milk; ordinary butcher paper; the plastic film used on packaged meats; or plastic produce bags from the supermarket.

Follow these helpful hints for freezing foods:

Freeze food quickly to 0° or below; post a dated list of food on the freezer door, and keep it current; use frozen food within 1 month to 6 weeks (Some seasonings become stronger while frozen, and some weaker. The degree of change is minimized if food is not left frozen too long); allow hot foods to cool to room temperature before freezing, then freeze them immediately; thaw, heat, and serve food in rapid succession. blanch or precook vegetables and drain them before freezing to stop enzyme action and to keep them from becoming discolored and mushy. (Drain blanched vegetables before freezing them.)

Thaw foods in the refrigerator or microwave whenever possible. Thawing in the refrigerator will take twice as long as on the counter, but it's much safer. Thawing time will vary according to the thickness or quantity of food in the container.

So many foods freeze well that it's more helpful to ask what doesn't freeze well than what does. Don't freeze the following foods. They will change color, texture, or separate in some way during the freezing or thawing process:

Raw salad vegetables (such as lettuce, radishes, tomatoes)

Raw eggs in their shells or hard-boiled eggs

Raw potatoes or boiled white potatoes (they turn black)

Commercial cottage cheese

Gelatin salads or desserts

Icing made with egg whites, boiled frostings, or cakes with cream fillings

Instant rice (it dissolves and becomes too mushy). You can freeze regular cooked rice.

Custard pies, cream pies, or pies with meringue

Index